D1294411

THE
MARSHALL CAVENDISH
ILLUSTRATED ENCYCLOPEDIA
OF
DISCOVERY
AND
EXPLORATION

The Taurus-Littrow region of the moon,
surveyed by the Apollo 17 mission.

THE
MARSHALL CAVENDISH
ILLUSTRATED ENCYCLOPEDIA
OF
DISCOVERY
AND
EXPLORATION

VOLUME 16

THE MOON AND BEYOND
Fred Appel and James Wollek

EDITORIAL COORDINATION
Beppie Harrison, John Mason
REVISION EDITOR
Donna Wood

Marshall Cavendish

New York · London · Toronto · Sydney

EDITORIAL STAFF
Executive Coordinators
Beppie Harrison
John Mason

Design Director
Guenther Radke

Editorial
Ann Craig
Maureen Matheson
Damian Grint
Lee Bennett
Marjorie Dickens
Jill Gormley
Isobel Campbell
Gail Roberts

Picture Editor
Peter Cook

Research
Ann Reading
Enid Moore
Sarah Waters
Margery MacLaren
Patricia Quick

Cartography
Geographical Projects

REVISION STAFF
Editor
Donna Wood

Editorial Director
Mark Dartford

Production Executives
Robert Paulley
John Collins

Editorial Contributors
Shane Winser
Robin Kerrod
Shane Roe

Art Editor
Janina Samoles

Picture Researcher
Moira McIlroy

Reference Edition Published 1990
© Marshall Cavendish Limited 1990
© J G Ferguson Publishing Company/Aldus Books Ltd. 1971

Published by Marshall Cavendish Corporation
147 West Merrick Road, Freeport, Long Island, NY11520

Printed by Mladinska knjiga, jugoslavija
Bound in Italy by L.E.G.O. S.p.A., Vicenza

Library of Congress Cataloging-in-Publication Data
Discovery and exploration.
  Summary: Describes the journeys of the world's explorers from the
first men who traveled beyond the then-known world to the scientific
explorations of today.
  ISBN 1-85435-114-1
  1. Discoveries (in geography) – Juvenile literature.
[1. Discoveries (in geography)   2. Explorers.]
G175, D57 1990
910'. 9 – dc20   89-15723
                                                                 CIP
                                                                  AC

ISBN 1-85435-135-4   The Moon and Beyond

Introduction

The dramatic saga of Man's exploration of his world; his courage and endurance against all odds, is expertly told in the seventeen volumes of the *Discovery and Exploration* encyclopedia.

The exploits of the first intrepid adventurers from Phoenicia, Greece and Rome on their perilous journeys into the unknown, exploration in the Dark Ages which ventured west to the Atlantic and across Asia to China, and the charting of the vast Pacific, a huge area of bleak, unyielding ocean from which many ships did not return, shows the determination of these early explorers in their search for even greater knowledge of the world about them.

Covered in these volumes are the oldest trades routes toward the spice and treasure of the Orient and the merchants who discovered them, the ruthless Conquistadors who put their thirst for gold above all else and the pioneering trappers and traders who were responsible for opening up North America. The motives of many of these men may have been purely mercenary, but we still owe them the debt of their discoveries, the roots of which still exist in customs and practices in many parts of the modern world to this day.

Painstakingly researched and minute in detail, these volumes of *Discovery and Exploration* contain a record of almost every important geographical discovery to take place in the history of mankind. Highly illustrated with a wealth of ancient documents, contemporary paintings, maps and illuminating extracts from the explorers' personal accounts of their journeys, these books make fascinating reading and are visually exciting; quite different from the dry works of reference that many of us are used to.

These are real adventure stories, telling of the explorers who broke through the barriers of their time regardless of personal hardship.

The later volumes move on in time to the great discoveries of the 17th, 18th and 19th centuries: the colonization and exploration of Australia and New Zealand, the taming of the Sahara and the unique challenge represented by Africa and Asia, lands of savagery and suffering to the often ill-prepared explorers of bygone days.

Some relatively recent exploration work occupies the final volumes of the set; the journeys to the North and South Poles, undersea exploration by pioneers like Jacques Cousteau, the endeavors of some famous mountaineers and, lastly, a history of man's foray into space and his achievements there. An 80 page Index volume completes the set.

Contents

**VOLUME 16
THE MOON AND BEYOND**

Hurricane Ellen over the Atlantic Ocean on September 20, 1973, pictured by Skylab 3.

Right: astronaut Garriot space-walking beside Skylab's telescope mount.

The New Frontier, Wherever It Is

1

Most early explorers knew only vaguely where their travels would take them and what problems and dangers they would have to face—many did not know at all. Columbus knew only that he wanted to travel west; the American pioneers headed westward too—or, as they expressed it, "thataway." The first polar explorers headed north or south. Once the early adventurer had gone beyond the limits of the known world, there were new and exciting discoveries to be made in almost any direction. The explorer could make his decision on the spot. He could go forward or back, north or south, east or west. There was new ground to be broken in any direction he chose to take.

Space, too, has a direction—up. But the 20th-century pioneer cannot just set off upward. Interplanetary space is, after all, what the word "space" implies—emptiness. In the vast nothingness of space, planets and their moons are few and far between. A man in a spacecraft moving at, say, a quarter of the speed of light, could travel for hundreds of years in many directions without encountering a single object larger than a stray dust particle or an atom or two.

The space explorer, however, has a problem no earlier pioneer had to deal with. The sun and its retinue are hurtling through space at inconceivable speeds. Nothing in space stands still relative to anything else—not even the earth or the moon. The space explorer must know precisely where he is going and exactly when he will get there. Because his target is also moving in space, probably at a higher speed than he is, he must study its path and speed of motion. Then he must plot a point in the great vastness of space where he and his target may meet at a given time. If he fails to keep his "appointment" or miscalculates his course by a tiny fraction of one degree, he may be lost in space forever.

There is more to this new kind of exploration, then, than simply heading "thataway." Before the space explorer sets out, he must know something about what the new frontier to be explored is. He must have an understanding of the scientific principles which govern its behaviour. It took man almost from the beginning of his existence until a few decades ago just to acquire the necessary knowledge to begin the exploration of space.

To early man, the earth was the whole universe; the sun was the chief god; and he explained the various other lights in the heavens as minor or attendant gods. Ancient man kept close watch over his gods in the sky and observed that many of them moved at regular intervals and often in regular paths. He used his observations to devise a number of excellent calendars. And he used these to predict, with remarkable

Above: ancient Egyptians believed the sun was a god, ferried daily across the sky in the company of a scarab.
Below: the Alexandrian astronomer, Ptolemy, in his *Geography*, underestimated the size of the ocean, which encouraged Columbus to start his famous voyage of discovery in 1492.

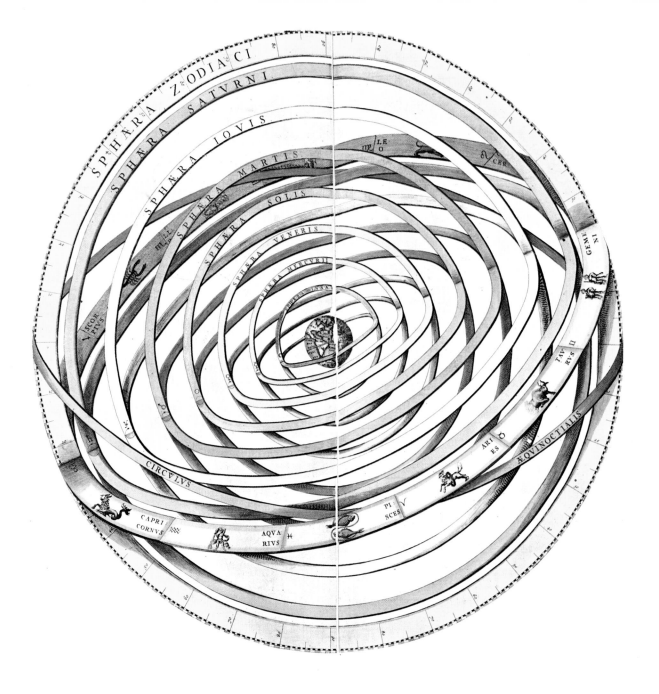

Above: a drawing of the 1600's decoratively demonstrates the astronomical theory of Ptolemy, with the earth as the center of the universe and all the other celestial bodies revolving around it.

Previous page: the progress of the moon across the sky — reported here by the camera — is caused as much by the movement of the earth in space (in this case its rotation) as by the moon itself.

accuracy, future movements of the same bodies. But he did not have any idea what or where the stars and planets were. However, he was certain that the vast, apparently motionless earth he knew was the center of all things. Thus he, quite reasonably, concluded that the lights in the sky, whatever they might be, revolved around the earth.

There is some doubt as to who was the first man to suggest that the earth was not the center of the universe, but it was probably Aristarchus of Samos, a Greek astronomer living about 270 B.C. Aristarchus believed that the earth revolved around the sun; that the sun was at rest; that the sun was larger than the earth; that the earth's rotation on its axis caused day and night; and that the changing seasons resulted from

the slant of the earth's axis to the plane of its orbit around the sun. Only one of Aristarchus' writings, *On the Sizes and Distances of the Sun and Moon*, survives today. It is from the comments of later astronomers, however, that we know of his theories.

We now know that Aristarchus was right, but his contemporaries did not think so. Instead, they preferred to rely on the authority of the great Greek scholar Aristotle, who had lived and worked a century before. Aristotle decreed that the earth was the center of the universe, and that it was stationary. His conclusions influenced the work of the astronomer, mathematician, and geographer whom we know as Ptolemy. Ptolemy lived and worked in Alexandria in about A.D. 150

Above: this map of the heavens, drawn in the 1600's, shows the solar system according to the Copernican theory, with the earth and other planets revolving around the sun. Note that at the time only six of the nine planets were known.

11

when Alexandria was a center of Greek learning. Two royal libraries were located there, and around them grew a great university which attracted some of the most important thinkers of the time.

The Ptolemaic system—as Ptolemy's explanation of heavenly motion is known today—placed the earth as the center of the universe with all other celestial bodies revolving around it in circular orbits. But careful observation showed Ptolemy and his followers that this could not be so. When viewed from earth, some of the planets seemed to move backward. To explain this and still hold to the theory of circular orbits, Ptolemy's system was revised to say that the planets themselves moved in small circles or *epicycles*, the centers of which moved around the earth in perfect circles. Whenever observed motions of celestial bodies did not agree with the basic theory, other epicycles were added to bring these exceptions into line. The Ptolemaic system was studied and accepted for about 1,400 years. Then a Polish astronomer, Nicolaus

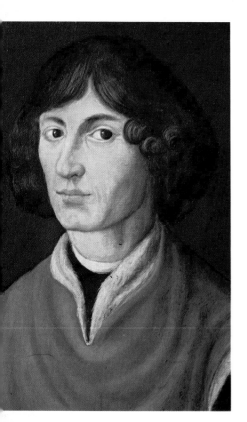

Left: Nicolaus Copernicus was the Polish astronomer who established by calculation that the Ptolemaic system did not adequately explain many facts that could be observed.

Right: Copernicus pursued his early studies at Krakow University, in Poland, where he organized his own theories that still form a basis for modern astronomy. The geometry room walls at Krakow still have the graceful designs that decorated them at the time Copernicus studied there.

"I, Galileo, son of the late Vincenzo Galilei, Florentine, aged seventy years, arraigned personally before this tribunal and kneeling before you, Most Eminent and Reverend Lord Cardinals Inquisitors-General against heretical depravity throughout the entire Christian commonwealth, having before my eyes, and touching with my hands the Holy Gospels, swear that I have always believed, do believe and by God's help will in the future believe all that is held, preached, and taught by the Holy Catholic and Apostolic Church. But, whereas, after an injunction had been judicially intimated to me by this Holy Office to the effect that I must altogether abandon the false opinion that the Sun is the center of the world and immovable and the Earth is not the center of the world and moves and that I must not hold, defend, or teach in any way whatsoever, verbally or in writing, the said false doctrine, and after it had been notified to me that the said doctrine was contrary to Holy Scripture, I wrote and printed a book in which I discuss this new doctrine already condemned and adduce arguments of great cogency in its favor without presenting any solution of these, I have been pronounced by the Holy Office to be vehemently suspected of heresy, that is to say, of having held and believed that the Sun is the center of the world and immovable and that the Earth is not the center and moves. Therefore, desiring to remove from the minds of your Eminences, and all faithful Christians, this vehement suspicion justly conceived against me, with sincere heart and unfeigned faith I abjure, curse, and detest the aforesaid errors and heresies and generally every other error, heresy, and sect whatsoever contrary to the Holy Church, and I swear that in future I will never again say or assert, verbally or in writing, anything that might furnish occasion for similar suspicion regarding me; but, should I know any heretic or person suspected of heresy, I will denounce him to this Holy Office or to the Inquisitor or Ordinary of the place where I may be. Further, I swear and promise to fulfil and observe in their integrity all penances that have been, or that shall be imposed upon me by this Holy Office. And in the event of my contravening (which God forbid!) any of these my promises and oaths, I submit myself to all the pains and penalties imposed and promulgated in the sacred canons and other constitutions, general and particular, against such delinquents. So help me God and these His Holy Gospels, which I touch with my hands."

So ran Galileo's words when in 1633 he denied, under pressure, his support of Copernicus. Although difficult to understand now, Galileo's choice to recant avoided martyrdom and gave him eight further years of life, which he used to help lay the foundations of modern physics.

Copernicus, produced the theories on which modern astronomy is based. In his *Concerning the Revolution of the Celestial Spheres,* published in 1543, Copernicus stated that the earth as well as the other planets revolved around the sun. At first, the Copernican system met with great resistance. This was partly because of the loyalty to Ptolemy that had built up over nearly 15 centuries, and partly because it was a blow to the ego of man in the 1500's to be told that his earth was not the center of the universe.

Fortunately for the progress of astronomy, proof of Copernicus' theories was soon to come from the Italian astronomer, mathematician, and physicist Galileo Galilei. In 1609, he heard reports from Holland about an optical magnifying device put together by a Dutch spectacle maker. Using this device, Galileo constructed the first complete astronomical telescope. It was capable of making objects appear 30 times nearer. With this telescope, Galileo observed the four moons of Jupiter on January 7, 1610. His discovery that the moons revolved around Jupiter, and not in epicycles that revolved around the earth, provided observational proof that the Ptolemaic theory was incorrect. In 1613, having made additional observations of the phases of Venus and of the sun, Galileo declared his allegiance to the denounced Copernican theory.

Old ideas die hard, however. In 1616, the papal court in Rome went so far as to declare the theories of Copernicus dangerous to the Roman Catholic faith. Galileo was summoned to Rome and ordered not to uphold, or to teach, the Copernican theory.

Defying the papal order, Galileo published a treatise, in 1632, concluding that Copernicus was correct. In 1633, he was again called to Rome and put on trial before the Inquisition. Under intense pressure, and perhaps torture, Galileo was made to recant all his "heretical" beliefs. He was first imprisoned, and then put under house arrest in his country villa until he died in 1642. But, despite the dangers and setbacks he suffered in his own lifetime, Galileo's discoveries could not be stifled and the Copernican theory eventually became accepted.

At about the same time that Galileo was making his studies in Italy, Tycho Brahe, the Danish astronomer, was laying the foundations for still more advances in the growing science of astronomy. For a while Brahe enjoyed the protection of the Danish king, who built an observatory for him. Brahe made thousands of precise plottings of the positions of stars and planets—most significantly, those of Mars. Despite his accurate observations of the solar system, Brahe never

Above: Brahe, a Danish astronomer, constructed his own observatory with the help of the Danish Royal Family. Below: Brahe produced a variation on the Copernican model; the sun revolving around the earth, planets around the sun.

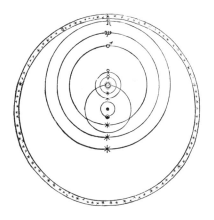

completely embraced the Copernican system. Instead he chose to work on the basis that the sun revolved around an immovable earth and the other five known planets revolved around the sun in circular orbits.

Brahe fell out of royal favor in 1597 and moved to Prague, where he established a new observatory in 1599. In the following year, he took on as an assistant a young German mathematics professor named Johannes Kepler. When Brahe died in 1601, he bequeathed his many calculations to Kepler. And it was Kepler's work on these calculations —over 300 years ago—that laid the groundwork for modern space exploration.

Kepler began plotting the various positions of Mars as observed by Brahe. But no matter how he modified the theory, no matter how hard he worked with epicycles on epicycles, he was unable to get his positions of Mars, as he observed and noted them, to conform to the Copernican theory of circular orbits. Then he made a vital discovery. If he plotted the positions of Mars in relation to the sun, ignoring preconceived notions, another figure emerged—the ellipse. The ellipse is a geometric figure with two focuses; the circle is merely a special ellipse in which both focuses are in the same place. Kepler found through further investigation that the orbits of planets are not circles, but ellipses in which the sun is always located at one of the two focuses. Known as Kepler's First Law, this rule is one of the most fundamental in all astronomy.

After this discovery, Kepler continued with his analysis of planetary motions. He noted that Mars moved faster when it was nearer the sun. How could this observation be expressed mathematically? He drew a line between the sun and one of the positions of Mars and then a second line between the sun and a succeeding position of Mars. He measured the area enclosed by each successive pair from the sun and the perimeter of the orbit. He did this several times along several positions of Mars at equal time intervals in its orbit. In each case, he found that although the distances between positions varied, Mars had swept over equal areas in equal times of travel. This is what we now call Kepler's Second Law.

In 1609, Kepler published Brahe's observations and calculations along with his own two laws. After further study, he published the third and last of his laws in 1619: The square of the period of each planet (the time it takes to make one revolution around the sun) is proportional to the cube of its mean distance from the sun. Thus, by comparing the period of Mars with the period of earth, Kepler could say Mars

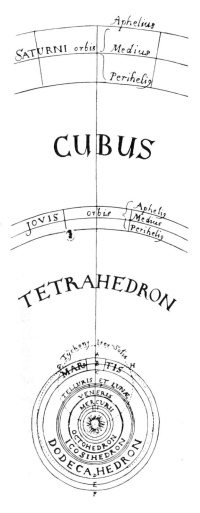

CUBUS

TETRAHEDRON

Left: Johannes Kepler (1571–1630).
Above: Kepler discovered that the planets move in elliptical orbits.
Below: Kepler's Second Law: the dotted line is Mars' orbit round the sun, with segments measured for comparison.

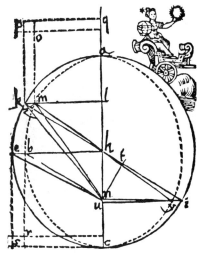

Above: Sir Isaac Newton, the English physicist and philosopher, discovered the law of gravity and showed its relationship to the orbits of the planets. Below: Newton's discovery was a major factor in the determination of the speed needed for a satellite to orbit earth.

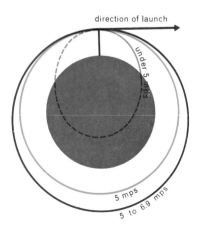

direction of launch

under 5 mps

5 mps

5 to 6.9 mps

was farther from the sun. So, although no one yet knew how far the distance between sun and earth is, the relative distance of the planets could be charted.

In less than a hundred years, the foundation of our understanding of the solar system had been laid. Copernicus described the system; Galileo proved him right by actual observation; and Kepler reduced to mathematics the precise motion of the planets, their satellites, and all other orbiting bodies.

Little more than half a century later, in 1687, Sir Isaac Newton, the English physicist and philosopher, worked out the theories which form the basis of our calculations on how man-made spacecraft could move outside the earth's atmosphere, and travel through outer space. During the course of this work, Newton built the first reflecting telescope.

Newton learned much from the work of Galileo and Kepler. From Kepler's laws and his own observations, he was able to formulate his Law of Universal Gravitation: All bodies in the universe, from the great stars and planets to the tiniest particles of dust, attract one another with a force that is proportional to the product of their masses and inversely proportional to the square of the distance between them.

Newton deduced this law primarily from a study of Kepler's Third Law, but a very ordinary occurrence was to crystallize his ideas on the problem of gravitation. According to legend, one day in 1665, when he was sitting in his garden, Newton saw an apple fall from a tree. He became convinced that, just as the apple is pulled toward earth, so is the moon. The same force which acts on the apple also retains the moon in orbit. The apple drops straight to earth, but, while the moon tends to move in a straight line, the gravitational force of the earth checks it just enough to cause it to move in a circular orbit. Newton went on to conceive the idea that a universal force, or gravitation, caused attraction between all bodies throughout the universe. He then deduced that the gravitational force between any pair of bodies in the universe can be measured by first calculating their relative weights and the distance between them.

It was not until about 1685 that Newton demonstrated these theories by calculation. During the 20 years that had passed after his initial discoveries, he had not made his ideas public. He felt that his theories were bound to meet with opposition, and he shunned criticism. Only the enthusiasm and encouragement of the English astronomer Edmund Halley eventually persuaded Newton to publish his theories. They

appeared in 1687, in a work entitled *Philosophiae Naturalis Principia Mathematica*—a book which has influenced the course of scientific thought right up to the present day.

Newton gave us another set of three laws—known now as Newton's Laws of Motion. Stated briefly, they are: (1) A body at rest tends to remain at rest and a body in motion tends to remain in motion at the same speed in a straight line, unless it is acted upon by some outside force. (2) Any change in a body's motion is proportional to the force acting on it and takes place in the direction in which the force is acting. (3) For every action, there is an equal and opposite reaction.

These three laws describe, among other things, all of the forces governing the motion of spacecraft in interplanetary space. Newton's law of gravitation tells us the effect on spacecraft of other bodies in space such as planets or moons. Kepler's laws tells us how a spacecraft and other bodies act when in orbit. By the end of the 1600's, man had all the basic information he needed to understand the motions of his targets in space and the forces required to get him to his rendezvous with them. It remained for him to find a vehicle that could use these forces to carry him into space.

Above: Woolsthorpe Manor, Lincolnshire where Newton is said to have realized that there was a force which made an apple fall to the ground. Below: the speeds necessary for an object to escape the earth's gravity, according to Newton and Kepler.

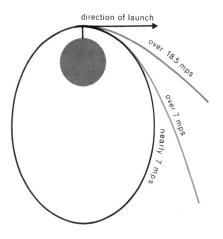

direction of launch

over 18.5 mps

over 7 mps

nearly 7 mps

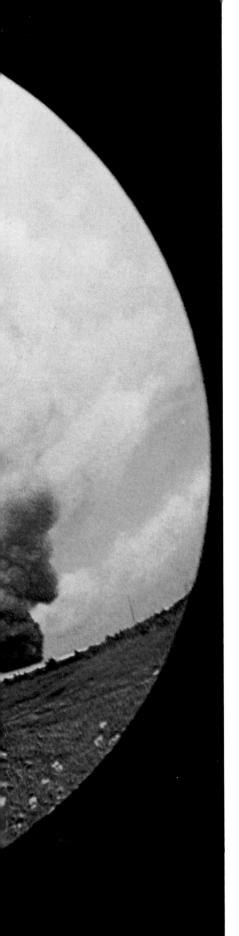

Getting into Space
2

Modern rocketry began in a Massachusetts cow pasture on March 16, 1926. On that frosty winter day, Robert Goddard launched the world's first liquid-fuel rocket. It rose to an altitude of 41 feet, traveled 184 feet down range, and reached a speed of nearly 60 miles an hour. Goddard considered that the launch was a great success.

Insignificant as this achievement might seem to us now, Goddard's rocket was an important step into the exploration of space. Before manned exploration of space could begin, it was necessary to find some way of lifting and propelling instruments out of the earth's atmosphere into the almost perfect vacuum of interplanetary space. All other propulsion devices capable of producing the necessary thrust need to "breathe" oxygen to do so. Only rockets that carry their own oxygen with them can meet the demands imposed by airless space.

But the development of rockets began long before man knew that there was any such thing as space or that he would have to use rockets to get there. Their earliest development was motivated by the desire for effective war-weapons. As far back as 1232, the Chinese, who had already invented gunpowder, used rockets against the invading Mongols. These rockets, described by writers of the time as "arrows of flying fire," seem to have been spears or arrows propelled by small sky-rockets. The secret of their manufacture did not remain long with

Left: the rocket is the only engine capable of propelling an object into space. This Saturn V was the launch vehicle that carried the Apollo astronauts to the moon in the 1960's and 1970's. But the dream of entering space and the experiments that led to the first rockets began centuries before.

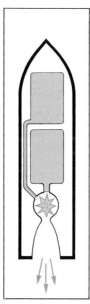

Right: illustrated here are the principles of two kinds of rocket. On the left is a solid-fuel rocket filled with propellant which burns to create hot gases which escape at the rear, producing thrust. In the liquid-fuel rocket on the right, the oxidizer (blue) and fuel (green) are kept in different tanks. They are pumped into the combustion chamber where they are ignited to produce gases that create the rocket's thrust.

the Chinese. Within a hundred years, war rockets had become a standard part of European army equipment and they were to remain so for three centuries or more. They were displaced by artillery that could be fired with greater accuracy—and which could cause considerably more damage to the enemy—than the unreliable rockets. By the late 1600's, rockets were used only in firework displays on feast days and national holidays.

However, about 150 years later, in the early 1800's, the war rocket returned to favor in Europe. The revival came about after British troops in India suffered a heavy defeat at the hands of Prince Hydar Ali of Mysore. The Prince's army used rockets in a series of victorious battles in 1790. His son improved on his father's rocket tactics and again dealt the British several more serious defeats in 1792 and 1799. When reports of these defeats reached England, military leaders began to look at rockets with renewed interest.

This period of rocket development is known as the "Congreve period." The name was that of a British colonel, Sir William Congreve, who was one of the more successful rocket experimenters of the time. Congreve never saw the Mysore rocket corps in action, but he studied several books and articles about the battles. He was sufficiently intrigued and impressed by what he read to begin experiments. In 1801 or 1802, he bought a number of large sky-rockets of the type used for firework displays. He tested them to find out what would have to be done to convert them into useful battle weapons. By 1805, Congreve had a war rocket ready to test against a real enemy. The British were fighting Napoleon's troops in Europe, and were eager to try out any new offensive weapons that might help them to victory over the French.

The first test on the field of battle, a rocket attack on the French port of Boulogne in late 1805, was a failure. But in the next year, the British again attacked Boulogne with rockets, and this time caused a devastating fire. Two years later, in 1807, another successful rocket attack against French troops in the Danish capital of Copenhagen, burned the city almost to the ground. Congreve's rockets were then employed successfully against the French armies in Danzig and Leipzig in 1813, and against the Americans in 1814 during the War of 1812. The familiar phrase in the U.S. national anthem, "the rockets' red glare," refers to a massive rocket bombardment of Fort McHenry in Baltimore. Congreve's rockets had proven their value in active service, and the other European military powers raced to develop their own rocket

Above: this original drawing shows "arrows of flying fire" rockets which were used by the Chinese as early as 1232 in their war against the Mongols.

Right: today sky-rockets are fired into the air for public amusement.

Left: Konstantin Tsiolkovsky.
Right: this drawing by Tsiolkovsky shows how he grappled with the problem of the enormous thrust required of a rocket to escape from the atmosphere and gravitational pull of the earth.

resources. Rockets were used as weapons through the major part of the 1800's, but by the end of the century were doomed yet again by advances in the development of artillery. The last use of the Congreve-type rockets was in 1881, in Russia.

Just about this time, also in Russia, the "golden age" of rocket research and discovery began. The period from about 1880 to the years immediately before the outbreak of World War II was dominated by three giants in the science of rocketry: Konstantin Tsiolkovsky, a Russian; the American Robert H. Goddard; and Hermann Oberth, a German.

Konstantin Tsiolkovsky was born near Moscow in 1857. When he was 10 years old he had a severe attack of scarlet fever and, although he recovered, the illness left him totally deaf. It may have been this handicap that turned his mind toward scientific research. In 1876, he became a high school teacher of mathematics and physics. At first his hobbies were concerned only with airships; then, later, he became fascinated by space travel. A paper he published in 1895 seems to mark the point in his life when he began to devote his full attention to the subject.

Unlike some earlier space prophets, Tsiolkovsky knew enough to appreciate the problems associated with space travel. He recognized that men would be able to travel in space only inside a sealed capsule that contained its own supplies of oxygen, water, food, and the other necessities of life. He also realized that some type of reaction engine—the rocket—would be necessary to make such a vehicle travel through space.

Tsiolkovsky carried his investigations further. He realized that the powder-propelled rockets of the time could never achieve the speeds he knew would be necessary to hurl man into space. He was well ahead of his time in concluding that these speeds would be achieved only in a rocket powered by a kerosene-type fuel—such as the ones that power today's rockets. Tsiolkovsky published his conclusions in a series of articles between 1903 and 1913, and later wrote a scientifically accurate novel about space travel. But his work did little to advance the science of rocketry in his own lifetime because his publications were not read outside Russia until after scientists in Western Europe and America had arrived at the same results independently. Then the Russian government had Tsiolkovsky's works translated and published abroad. It took other scientists reaching the same conclusions and building on his ideas to bring modern space travel nearer.

Above: the Congreve rocket. It was named after Sir William Congreve, an English colonel, who re-awakened military interest in rockets in the 1800's.

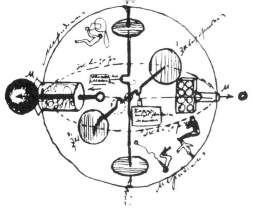

Below: Tsiolkovsky (1857–1935) worked in this study in his house in Kaluga, about 100 miles south of Moscow. Here he presented his conclusions which were published in a series of articles, the first scientific papers on the use of rockets for spaceflight.

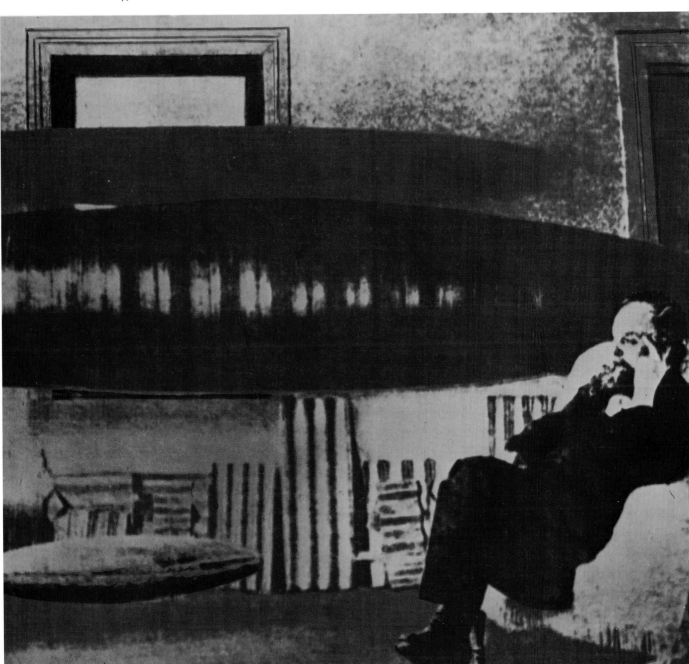

In the United States, the pioneer scientist was Robert Hutchings Goddard, "the father of American rocketry." Goddard was a professor of physics at Clark University, Worcester, Massachusetts. He had been a rocket enthusiast since his school days. In 1916, he submitted a highly technical study of rocket potential to the Smithsonian Institution in an appeal for research funds. As a result, he received $5,000 to conduct additional experiments. In 1919, the Smithsonian published a 69-page pamphlet of Goddard's entitled "A Method of Reaching Extreme Altitudes." It dealt mainly with the possibility of carrying weather-research instruments to higher altitudes than the 20-mile limit of the sounding balloons then in use. Goddard also suggested the possibility that a long-range rocket might fly to the moon carrying a quantity of flash powder that would explode on impact, making a display that could be observed from earth. However, this suggestion brought Goddard much unwelcome publicity in the newspapers and was instrumental in leading him to conduct his subsequent experiments in relative secrecy.

Like Tsiolkovsky, Goddard realized that liquid-fuel rockets would have to be used to improve rocket performance. For his own experiments he used a mixture of gasoline and liquid oxygen. In November 1923, Goddard fired on a test stand what was probably the first liquid-fueled rocket motor in the world. After additional experiments, he put

Left: Robert Goddard has been called "the father of American rocketry" for his pioneer work in the use of liquid fuels. He was the first scientist to prove that a rocket works in a vacuum.

Right: much of his later work was done privately in New Mexico, where he launched a rocket that reached a record height of 7,500 feet. After his death, NASA named its center in Maryland the Goddard Space Flight Center.

one of his motors in a rocket, and, on March 16, 1926, made the first successful launch.

Goddard continued his experiments at Auburn, Massachusetts. But he ran into trouble with the local fire marshal, who was convinced that one of Goddard's rockets would eventually cause a forest fire. Fortunately Goddard received $100,000 grant from the aviation philanthropist, Daniel Guggenheim. This enabled him to move to the Mescalero ranch near Roswell, New Mexico, where he was able to continue his research in private.

Goddard made many important contributions to rocket research in the years he spent at Roswell. In 1932, he flew the first rocket stabilized by gyroscopically controlled vanes. And in 1935, he launched

a rocket to the record altitude of 7,500 feet. In many of his rockets, Goddard made use of a number of extremely advanced techniques, among them a method of cooling the motor's combustion chamber using the fuels themselves.

The third rocket giant of the time was Hermann Oberth, born in the old Austro-Hungarian Empire in 1894. Unlike Goddard he was a theorist rather than a builder or experimenter: he never actually built or flew any rockets. However, he did work more publicly than his American counterpart. He also associated with a group of rocket enthusiasts who provided him with the practical knowledge he lacked. Oberth became a professor of physics and mathematics in Germany and, in 1923, published a book about space travel. Interest in this, and in his

Above: Goddard (left) with three of his assistants at work on a rocket with the casing removed in their workshop at Roswell, New Mexico. Choosing to work away from the public eye, this team used some considerably advanced techniques in their researches, and the contribution they made to the American space program cannot be overestimated.

29

work, led to the formation of the most important rocket movement in Europe—the German Society for Space Travel. The members of this society helped develop the V-2 in World War II.

In his book, *The Rocket into Interplanetary Space,* Oberth discussed many technical problems of spaceflight. He claimed that scientific and technical knowledge was sufficient to construct rockets capable of climbing above the earth's atmosphere. He maintained that future rockets would be able to escape from the earth into interplanetary space, and he was convinced that rockets would one day be able to carry men safely into space. He gave—in some detail—his specifications for the rockets and spaceships that would be able to do precisely what he predicted. While these were not blueprints for space vehicles, Oberth's book provided a theoretical basis from which engineering models could be drawn. It also laid the cornerstone for the research that would finally lead to the modern rocket.

Surprisingly, even though it was so technical, Oberth's book was a big success. It excited the imagination of the European public. Soon rocket societies for the promotion of interplanetary travel were formed all over Europe, particularly in Germany. Previously, rocket enthusiasts had been regarded as eccentrics and dreamers. After Oberth, the societies numbered among their members some of the most respected names in the European scientific community. Rocketry had attained respectability at last; the kind of respectability that brought it public tolerance, government cooperation, and, in many cases, financial support.

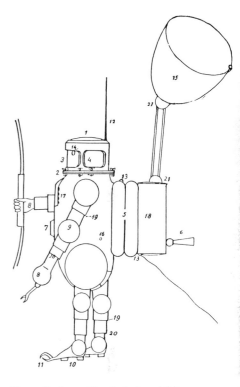

Above: Professor Oberth designed this space-suit long before man went into space.

1. Entrance hatch
2. Flange
3. & 4. Window
5. Receptacle for compressed air, oxygen, fuel for repulsion pistol
6. Repulsion pistol
7. Switch box
8. Glove and pick-off attachment
9. Linkages
10. Magnet for adhesion
11. Pick-off attachment
12. Short-wave antenna
13. Hook for hanging
14. Rear vision mirror
15. Dissipation of heat
16. Plug connection for phone
17. Hinge for trace goggle
18. Gas cylinder
19. Place for shortening linkages
20. Hinge joint
21. Swivel for dissipation of heat

Left: a set for the 1929 movie, "Girl in the Moon," which Oberth designed. He actually built a rocket for the film, but was unable to make it fly.

The Modern Rocket
3

In January, 1933, Adolf Hitler took control of Germany, promising to rebuild Germany's military might. The peace treaties signed at the end of World War I had forbidden the rearmament of Germany. Later on Hitler was to ignore these restrictions, but in 1933 war rockets seemed a good starting point for rearmament because the treaties specifically prohibited only conventional weapons. In addition, there was at the time intense interest in rockets among German space travel societies. As a result Hitler was able to lead Germany into a major effort in the development of rockets. By 1937, with war clouds already gathering over Europe, German rocketry had advanced enough for a top-secret laboratory to be established at Peenemünde, a tiny fishing village in northern Germany on the coast of the Baltic Sea.

Heading the Peenemünde project was Major General Dr. Walter Dornberger. To take advantage of the knowledge and experience civilian rocket societies had gained before the rise of Hitler, the army also hired for the scheme a young rocket enthusiast and engineer named Wernher von Braun. Eventually the Peenemünde project employed an estimated 20,000 scientists, engineers, technicians, and workmen. While Hitler and his generals were interested only in developing more and more deadly weapons of war, many of the scientists worked on the project more out of a genuine passion for rocketry than out of any strong concern for the German war effort.

Peenemünde is significant in the history of rocketry because it was there that the prototypes of the first modern rockets were built. In the course of work there, many false starts were made, many unproductive

Left: the team of men were established in a secret rocket base at Peenemünde on the Baltic coast. This reconnaissance picture, taken by the RAF at the end of 1943, was the first glimpse the outside world had of the installation.

Right: Hitler, here with Goebbels on his left, assembled a brilliant team of scientists, engineers and technicians to develop rockets as weapons.

Above: the V-1 "rockets," here being wheeled to the launch pad, were 25 feet 4 inches long and carried one ton of explosives. The British called them *buzz-bombs* because the engine was heard before the rocket was seen.

avenues of research were explored and then abandoned, and the directions for future rocket development were finally established.

The Peenemünde scientists perfected a number of different weapons, most notably the V-1, the *doodle-bug* or *buzz-bomb*—so named because of the noise of its engine—and the V-2 guided missile. Both were launched against England during World War II, causing widespread devastation and the loss of thousands of lives. Although commonly thought of as a rocket, the V-1 was a flying bomb propelled by a jet engine. The engine "breathed" air instead of carrying its own oxygen supply with it. As such, it was not a rocket, but a pilotless jet airplane that could travel a distance of about 150 miles at 360 miles per hour.

The V-2, on the other hand, was the first modern rocket. It stood about 46 feet high and weighed in total some 12 tons, of which $8\frac{1}{2}$ tons was fuel and oxidizer. When fired, the rocket rose vertically and then tilted to a 45° angle on a trajectory that carried it 60 miles above the earth, and a horizontal distance of 200 miles from its firing point. The V-2 burned a combination of alcohol and liquid oxygen. The fuel was contained in two tanks located between the rocket motor and the one-ton warhead. The fuel was pumped into the rocket motor by steam-driven turbines of a type still in use today.

The V-2 utilized many of the devices contained in today's rockets. Among its instruments were gyroscopes that stabilized high-altitude flight by controlling the movement of vanes introduced into its exhaust blast. The rocket had external fins that helped to stabilize it in the lower atmosphere, just as an arrow's feathers do. But in the thinner air of the upper atmosphere, these fins became useless. The internal vanes that

Above: the V-1 was a German missile regulated by both a magnetic compass and a clock mechanism. The missile flew toward England, and after a certain time the clock locked the missile's controls and crash-dived it into the ground.

Left: the V-1 was powered by a pulsejet engine and could travel about 150 miles at a speed of 360 mph. The British Royal Air Force, defending the skies over England, with Spitfires (seen above a V-1 in this picture) and Hurricanes, were able to shoot down the *buzz-bombs* in large numbers. However, thousands of civilians were killed by the bombs.

Above: when the V-2 guided missile reached high altitudes the external fins did not maintain the flight path, so a gyroscope was employed to control vanes in the exhaust that directed the rocket blast on the correct course.

redirected the rocket blast were crucial in controlling the flights of the V-2 and other high-altitude rockets.

Other major V-2 innovations concerned the cooling of the rocket motor. It had become obvious to the rocket-builders that something would have to be done to prevent the tremendous heat generated by the burning fuels from destroying the rocket motor. They found that this could be accomplished in two ways: first, the alcohol fuel, on its way into the combustion chamber of the motor, was directed through channels between the inner and outer walls of the motor. This tended to cool the walls of the motor so that it was not destroyed by the heat inside. Secondly, while most of the alcohol fuel was directed to the 18 burner cups at the top of the combustion chamber, some of it was channeled so as to spray directly into the exhaust blast at the rocket's throat. In the past, this had been the part that most often burned out. The exhaust blast pressed the cold alcohol against the nozzle wall where

Above: this V-2 being launched at
Peenemünde was destined for London.
Despite its dreadful purpose, the
development of the V-2 contributed
enormously to the advance of rocket
techniques.

it formed a cool protective film, partially shielding the wall from the heat of the blast. Both processes helped to make possible the use of the fuels that burn at such tremendously high temperatures in modern rockets.

As the German war effort began to turn sour in late 1944, it became clear to the scientists at Peenemünde that their laboratory would eventually fall to the Russian army closing in on northern Germany from the east. The American and British armies would be moving in from the west. Many of the scientists felt it would be far better to be captured by the British and Americans than by the Russians.

So, while the laboratory at Peenemünde was kept in operation by technicians right up until the date of its capture, most of the scientists, including many of those who had been recruited from the rocket societies of the early 1930's, quietly slipped away. They made for territory they knew was likely to be captured by the Americans and the

British. One of the major factories for the production of V-2 missiles was also located in territory that was taken by the Americans in the great Allied military drive that ended the war in Europe.

Peenemünde fell on May 5, 1945, to Russian infantry under the command of Major Anatole Vassilov. The major later reported that on arrival at the laboratory he found nearly 75 per cent wreckage, very little salvageable equipment, and very few skilled personnel. The rocket-men had moved out.

The V-2 factory captured by the Americans was scheduled to be turned over to the Russians. Before making the transfer, however, the Americans removed 300 box-car loads of V-2 missiles, parts, and equipment. Most of the top Peenemünde scientists managed to reach territory under British or American protection and were transferred to the United States in a secret operation code-named "Operation Paperclip." In effect, Peenemünde, or a large part of it, moved from the Baltic coast of Germany to the American southwestern desert at White Sands, New Mexico.

This proving ground, established only five months earlier, was a desolate desert valley 120 miles long and 40 miles wide situated not far from the site of Goddard's laboratory. The first U.S. modified V-2 took off from White Sands on April 16, 1946. The United States' "big rocket" program had begun. Peenemünde's V-2 was the seed from which the giant space rockets of both the United States and the Soviet Union first sprang. In the decade leading up to the Soviet Union's dramatic launching of Sputnik 1 on October 4, 1957, the United States and the Soviet Union forged ahead on their big rocket programs. They both built largely on captured German rockets and technology. The early flights of the V-2 had paid off to some extent in the knowledge and experience needed for man's step into space.

By the 1940's, men had already collected a sizable amount of the theoretical and practical information they needed to put them on their way to the frontier of space. Newton and Kepler and other astronomers had described the motions of the heavenly bodies and the forces that caused their movements. Rocket experimenters, through much trial and error, had produced rockets that worked; that could rise to greater and greater heights; that were increasingly controllable from the earth; and that could carry heavier and heavier payloads. Pioneers such as Tsiolkovsky, Goddard, and Oberth had written about the possibilities of space travel and stated some of the principles that would lead to these possibilities becoming reality. But space travel

Above: when it became clear that Peenemünde would fall to the Russians, the German personnel almost completely destroyed the rocket laboratory. The photo shows the ruins found by the Russian army.

Right: hoping the Americans would enable them to continue their work, many of the Peenemünde scientists, including Wernher von Braun, seen here just after his "capture," made their way toward American-held territory.

39

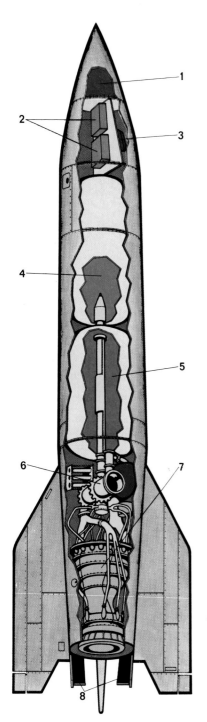

1. Payload (explosives)
2. Automatic pilot
3. Steering gyroscope
4. Fuel: ethyl alcohol
5. Oxidizer: liquid oxygen
6. Turbopumps
7. Combustion chamber
8. Exhaust vanes

Left: the V-2 was a pre-set missile with more than a ton of explosives. Guided by an automatic pilot, it could travel a distance of about 200 miles at a speed of 3,600 mph, much faster than the speed of sound.

was not yet a fact. Before it could become so, it needed the additional flight experience and theoretical work after World War II to bring the new frontier within reach.

Put at its simplest, research still had to discover what it would take, in terms of rocket size and rocket power, to put a satellite or a man into space. The first essential was to find out how a man-made machine could escape the grasp of the earth's gravity. Newton's Law states that gravity diminishes with the square of the distance from an object. From this it can be derived mathematically that gravitational pull extends out into space to infinity although at substantial distance the pull becomes very small. In order to overcome this pull, a rocket produces a pushing force called *thrust* which, like weight, can be measured in pounds. The rocket must have a thrust greater than its own weight and the weight of the satellite or spacecraft put together. The vital question then arises: How fast does the rocket have to travel to overcome the force of gravity? Scientists made all the necessary calculations, and found a rocket would need a speed—a velocity—of about 7 miles

per second (i.e., about 25,000 miles per hour) to escape. These figures
do not account for the effect of air resistance and the diminishing power
of the force of gravity as a body rises to great altitudes. They were,
however, a good rough indicator to the magnitude of the necessary
escape velocity.

How could a rocket be made to achieve speed of that order? Perhaps
the most important single consideration, experts agreed, was the rocket
fuel (otherwise termed the *propellant*) because the amount of energy
each pound of fuel could release would be vital. Scientists express this
quantity as the *specific impulse* of a fuel. Surprisingly, perhaps, to
a non-scientist, most explosives have specific impulses inferior to
those of ordinary fuels such as gasoline. Explosives burn fast and
release all their energy at once, which is undesirable in rocket flight.
Today, the highest specific impulse rocket fuels are liquids such as
alcohol, hydrazine, and liquid hydrogen.

Having established the specific impulse of his chosen fuel, the
scientist next has to determine the "mass ratio" of the rocket. The mass

ratio determines the final velocity attainable by the rocket in terms of
its exhaust velocity. The mass ratio is the weight of the rocket when
it is filled to capacity with fuel divided by its weight after it has burned
all its fuel.

As an example, if a rocket weighs 12 tons fully fueled and 4 tons
empty, its mass ratio would be 3 : 1.

Space scientists discovered that for a rocket to achieve its own
exhaust velocity—that is, for the rocket's upward speed to equal the
speed of the gases moving out of its nozzle—the rocket's mass ratio
had to be at least 2.7 : 1, no matter what type of fuel was used.

In other words if the weight of a loaded rocket is 270 pounds, 27,000
pounds, or even 270 tons, its final speed will equal the exhaust velocity
of the fuel being used if the empty rocket weighs 100 pounds, 10,000
pounds or 100 tons respectively. The scientists also found that a rocket
could be made to achieve twice its exhaust velocity by simply squaring
the mass ratio (2.7 × 2.7)—i.e., 7.3 : 1. And they could make it attain
three times its exhaust velocity by cubing that mass ratio, i.e. by giving
it a mass ratio of about 20 : 1.

As a result, once a scientist knows the exhaust velocity of the most
powerful rocket fuel he has available and once he knows the velocity
he wants his rocket to attain, he has a clear view of the engineering
problem before him. He knows what the mass ratio of his rocket must
be to make the speed of the rocket equal to the exhaust speed of the fuel.
He must attempt to keep to that ratio by holding down the combined
weight of his payload and rocket dead weight, i.e. the unrelieved weight
of the rocket when inert.

The development of the step principle, or multi-stage rocket, however, made the space scientist's job just a little easier. Experimentation
with multi-stage rockets revealed a remarkable effect on required
mass ratios.

To compute the mass ratio of the entire assembly, the mass ratios of
the individual rockets in the assembly were multiplied. In other words,
if there were two rockets, each with a mass ratio of 2.7, mounted on
top of each other, the mass ratio of the two-stage rocket was 2.7 × 2.7,
or 7.3 : 1—the mass ratio required for the second stage to achieve its
exhaust velocity. It soon became apparent that unless some new,
phenomenally powerful fuel combinations were discovered, future
space rockets would have to be multi-stage vehicles utilizing this
multiplication of mass ratios to reach the required escape velocities.
And that has been the pattern ever since.

The First Steps into Space
4

After World War II the Soviet Union launched a major program to develop large liquid-fuel rockets—"transatlantic rockets," as Stalin called them—capable of delivering a nuclear warhead anywhere around the globe. The United States preferred to await the development of smaller nuclear weapons requiring smaller rockets. This difference in approach gave the Soviet Union a critical early lead in the space race, although the full extent of the Soviet lead was not to become apparent to the West for some time.

Another factor in United States rocket development was rivalry between the Army, Navy and Air Force, all of whom produced their own rockets for various purposes. In 1950, the United States Army transferred its team of German V-2 scientists from White Sands to the Redstone Arsenal in Huntsville, Alabama. There, under Wernher von Braun, a 200-mile range missile was developed, named the Redstone. It made its first flight in August 1953.

The next significant American missile of the period was the Air Force's Atlas, which produced 367,000 pounds of thrust and had a range of 9,000 miles In late 1955 and early 1956, work was also begun on two intermediate-range—1,800 miles—missiles, the Air Force's Thor and the Army's Jupiter, the latter developed by Wernher von Braun's team at the Redstone Arsenal.

Events came to a head with the International Geophysical Year (IGY), scheduled to run from July, 1957 to December, 1958. The IGY was to be a time of worldwide scientific cooperation in study of the earth, the atmosphere, and the sun.

One of the grandest schemes envisaged for the IGY was the launching of a man-made satellite into orbit around the earth. Scientists would learn much simply by observing it in orbit: how it reacted to small differences in the gravity of the earth, how long it took to fall out of orbit, and so on.

In 1955, the United States announced that during the IGY it would attempt to launch a series of small, unmanned, earth-circling satellites. A few days later, Soviet space expert Leonid Sedov stated that the U.S.S.R. would also launch satellites during the IGY, and that these

An important development in space rocketry was the Atlas ballistic missile. This rocket was originally designed to carry a nuclear warhead, but was later used to launch the Mercury one-man spacecraft into orbit around the earth, as shown in this photograph.

45

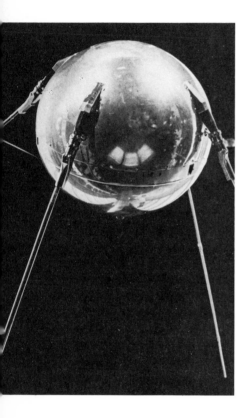

Above: the world's first satellite, Sputnik 1, launched by Russia on October 4, 1957, during the International Geophysical Year.

would be much bigger than the proposed American satellites. The space race was on.

The Soviet Union planned to use one of its large, intercontinental missiles, then under development, to launch its earth satellite. The United States decided instead to develop a new launcher called Vanguard, based on rockets designed and built by the Navy—a decision which lost them the space race. On October 4, 1957, before Vanguard had even been test fired, the Soviet Union launched a 184-pound satellite named Sputnik 1 into orbit around the earth (the name Sputnik means "travelling companion"). Sputnik 1 carried a radio transmitter which sent out "beep-beep" signals, allowing scientists to track it and to learn about the nature of the upper ionosphere. A month later the Soviet Union achieved an even more spectacular success with the launch of Sputnik 2, a half-ton craft carrying the dog Laika. In May 1958, came Sputnik 3, weighing over one ton, packed with scientific equipment.

In the United States, Sputnik 1 triggered a vast emotional reaction. The Russian achievement was a blow to the national pride, almost a national humiliation. The American space program was at once given top priority, and in December, 1957, the Project Vanguard team announced that it would attempt to launch an instrument-package into orbit on December 6. But, on the day, after the rocket ignited, the Viking first stage exploded and the rocket collapsed in flames.

The United States, however, had a second rocket. After the success of Sputnik 1, Wernher von Braun had been authorized to construct a modified version of the Redstone rocket called Juno 1. On January 31, 1958—just 84 days after von Braun had been given the go-ahead—the Juno 1 boosted a 31-pound, pencil-shaped satellite, Explorer 1, into orbit from Cape Canaveral in Florida. The United States was back in the space race.

Among the 18 pounds of instruments on Explorer 1 was an experiment designed by James Van Allen, a physicist from the University of Iowa. The experiment detected a huge, hitherto unknown and unexpected doughnut-shaped zone of intense radiation girdling the earth—subsequently named the Van Allen Radiation Belt. Its discovery is considered to be one of the major scientific "finds" of the space age.

On March 17, 1958, a Vanguard rocket finally succeeded in boosting a $3\frac{1}{4}$-pound grapefruit-sized package into orbit. From variations in its orbit, geophysicists were able to discover that the earth is slightly pear-shaped, not a flattened sphere as had been thought.

The next years were years of intensive space research and development for both nations. By 1961, a total of 42 instrument-packages had gone into space, 9 Russian and 33 American. Vanguard 2 (American) became the first weather satellite. Luna 1 (Russian) made the first close pass of the moon. Discoverer 1 (American) achieved the first near-polar orbit. Pioneer 5 (American) explored the space between earth and Venus. Tiros 1 (American) sent back the first pictures of the earth's surface and cloud cover to be used in forecasting weather. Luna 2 became the first man-made object to hit the moon and Luna 3 sent back the first pictures of the back of the moon. The United States launched Echo 1, the world's first communications satellite.

As 1961 began, it was obvious that the time was near when man would at last enter space. In the previous year, the Russians had orbited and attempted to recover three man-sized capsules. The first attempt, in May, 1960, had failed. The second, on August 19, had resulted in the first recovery of live creatures from space, the dogs Belka and

Above: on January 31, 1958, the Americans' first satellite was blasted into space by a four-stage rocket. Called Explorer 1, it carried scientific experiments including one which discovered the Van Allen Radiation Belt. The belt, consisting of electrically charged particles trapped in the earth's magnetic field, begins about 500 miles above the equator and extends out into space about 40,000 miles.

Left: Major Yuri Gagarin was the first man in space. On April 12, 1961, he successfully completed one orbit of the earth in his spaceship, Vostok 1, before landing safely near Saratov in European Russia.

Strelka. On a third attempt, December 2, the ship's retrorockets had failed to fire and the spacecraft had burned up on re-entry into the atmosphere.

For the initial United States manned flight the plan was to utilize a modified Redstone missile, the Mercury-Redstone, topped with a cone-shaped, one-man Mercury capsule. A Mercury-Redstone carrying the chimpanzee Ham blasted off from Cape Canaveral at five minutes before noon on January 31, 1961. The capsule was recovered safely and Ham was eating an apple on the flight deck of the recovery aircraft carrier only a little over an hour after his flight into space had begun.

As tests of the Mercury-Redstone rocket went ahead, the United States was testing a second space rocket, the Mercury-Atlas. The first man-in-space flight would be suborbital: the spaceship, launched by Redstone, was scheduled to go up and come down but not to go into orbit. Only after up-and-down flights had been shown to be successful would the powerful Atlas rocket be used to put a man into orbit.

Once again, the superiority of Soviet launch rockets proved crucial. On March 9, the Russians launched a dog, Chernushka, into orbit and successfully recovered her after one orbit around the earth. This spacecraft weighed 10,364 pounds, compared with the American Mercury capsule's weight of about 3,000 pounds. On March 25, another dog, Zvesdochka, was blasted into orbit and was later recovered alive and well along with the capsule.

Then on April 10, foreign correspondents in Moscow reported rumours sweeping the city that the Russians had put a man into orbit. There was no official confirmation that day or the next. But, on April 12, the official Soviet news agency *Tass* issued the following announcement:

"The world's first spaceship Vostok, with a man on board, has been launched on April 12 in the Soviet Union on a round-the-earth orbit. The first space navigator is Soviet citizen pilot Major Yuri Alexseyevich Gagarin. Bilateral radio communication has been established and is being maintained with Gagarin."

48

Above: a Vostok rocket, the vehicle that sent Gagarin into space, on the launch pad ready for liftoff. Gagarin's flight, on April 12, 1961, was a great triumph for the U.S.S.R., proving that the Soviet achievements remained ahead of those of the U.S.A.

Left: the news that a man had at last been launched into space made head-lines in newspapers all around the world.

Man had entered space and safely returned. The details—or some of them—emerged later. After one orbit and 108 minutes of flight in space in his Vostok spaceship, Yuri Gagarin landed safely near the Volga River, some 15 miles south of the city of Saratov.

Gagarin was 27 years old and weighed 154 pounds. His Vostok spacecraft weighed 10,417 pounds.

It was later established that the spacecraft's two-stage booster had been fired from the Baikonur Cosmodrome east of the Aral Sea near the town of Tyuratum. It attained an orbit with an apogee (high point) of 203 miles and a perigee (low point) of 112 miles. The orbit was inclined 65 degrees to the equator. Gagarin experienced approximately 89 minutes of weightlessness during his 108-minute flight.

"May I go first?"
—Yuri Gagarin

Fifteen miles south of the town of Engel's in the Saratov region of the U.S.S.R., Anna Timofeyevna Takhtarova, a forester's wife, and her six-year-old daughter Rita were attending to a calf in a clearing not far from the village of Smelovka. It was April 12, 1961, 10:55 A.M. Moscow time. Suddenly the girl pointed skyward. Above them a parachute was blossoming downward. As it came nearer the two could see a blackened metal object dangling from the shrouds. It landed with a light bump a few dozen yards from a deep ravine. As the woman and girl watched in nervous trepidation, a figure started to walk toward them—a man dressed in a bright orange suit with a metal helmet. The man was Russian cosmonaut Major Yuri Alexseyevich Gagarin, the first human being to experience the miracle of spaceflight.

Gagarin remembered that moment: "Stepping out onto firm ground, I caught sight of a woman and a little girl standing near a dappled calf and looking curiously at me. I went toward them and they moved forward to meet me. The closer they got, however, the slower their steps became. I was still in my bright orange spacesuit and they were a bit frightened by its strangeness."

At that moment a group of tractor drivers who had been working near by rushed over. "Yuri Gagarin! Yuri Gagarin," shouted one of them. Gagarin stepped into the open welcoming arms of the tractor driver—in a traditional Russian greeting.

Yuri Gagarin was born in the Smolensk region, the son of a poor peasant, in 1934. As a schoolboy one of his favorite authors was the science-fiction prophet H. G. Wells. And it was while studying at technical school in Saratov that he joined the local flying club. He remembered the first time he was allowed to fly alone: "I was in raptures. Only pilots can understand what feeling one has during one's first solo flight."

The young Yuri had made his mind up: he would become a fighter pilot. He was still in training when the Russians launched the first earth satellite—the famous Sputnik—in 1957. "I

felt a light, already familiar chill," he recalled. "Was it then that I developed the wish to fly in space?" Two years later he was one of 12 men chosen to be trained as cosmonauts.

Fellow cosmonaut Gherman Titov—the second Russian in space—remembered Gagarin in training . . . "constantly ready to undergo the hardest tests. Whether it was a question of exercises in weightless conditions, staying for long periods of time in the soundproof chamber or parachute jumping, he would always say: 'May I go first?'" Gagarin passed the training period with flying colors—and it was he who was finally selected to be the first man in space.

On the morning of April 12, 1961, at the launching site of Baikonur, Gagarin was awoken at 5:30 A.M. After a pre-flight medical check he began to dress in his spacegear. "I first put on a warm, soft, sky-blue set of lightweight overalls," he remembers. "My comrades then started helping me to get into my protective bright orange spacesuit which would enable me to work even if the cabin was depressurized." After the instruments on the spacesuit had been checked, Gagarin donned a white headphone set and the pressure helmet of his spacesuit. He had a final discussion with his doctor and then signed autographs.

Finally the word came. Gagarin boarded a bus to take him to Vostok 1: "I could already see the silver body of the rocket pointing at the sky in the distance. It looked like a giant beacon and the first ray of the rising sun shone on its pointed peak."

On the launching pad Gagarin turned for a moment and lifted his arm: "Goodbye earth," he called out. "Goodbye friends." The lift ride to the top platform took two minutes. A hatch in the side of the Vostok space vehicle was opened and Gagarin climbed in. He remembers that moment: "I got into the cabin, which smelt of country air. I was helped into my seat and the hatch was then silently closed. I was left alone with the controls."

At exactly 9:07 A.M. Moscow time, the engines of the booster rocket roared into life. It paused for a second or two and trembled a little before disappearing behind a raging storm of flame. Then it was gone—leaving a fiery track against the sky.

Inside the cabin Gagarin heard a whistle and an ever-growing din. "The gigantic rocket trembled all over. The powerful motors made the music of the future. The G-loads (gravity) began to get heavier. I felt an insuperable force pressing me harder and harder into my seat. I found it difficult to move my hands and feet."

At 9:10 the cone separated from the booster rocket and Gagarin reported that he could see the earth through his porthole. "It's beautiful, beautiful."

At 9:12 the second stage separated and for the first time Gagarin reported the curvature of the earth. "The horizon," he said, "tends a bit downwards."

By 9:13 Vostok was in orbit. The ground controllers leapt out of their seats and congratulated each other with hugs and kisses. Gagarin reported that he could see mountains and forests through the earth's cloud cover. And he reported something else: for the first time a human being was experiencing the weightlessness of space. He was enjoying the experience: "Weightlessness is having a pleasant effect on me," he radioed. "Nothing at all the matter with it."

Later he recalled that the weightlessness had played a cruel trick on him. "After making a note in the log book, I let go of the pencil and it floated off freely in the cabin, together with the clipboard. The knot in the cord attaching it to the board came unexpectedly undone, however, and it dived under my seat. For the rest of the time I had to transmit my observations over the radio and record them on tape."

At 9:57 Vostok flew over America—and Gagarin found himself thinking of American astronaut Alan Shepard who eventually followed him into space a month later. "For some reason I imagined Alan Shepard would be the one to do this."

At 10:06 he reported that he could see the earth's horizon, which he described as a "very beautiful sort of halo; a rainbow from the top of the earth downwards." On the other side of the Vostok he could see "stars going by. It's a very beautiful sight."

Three minutes later Gagarin saw the first sunrise from space. Later he recalled: "I thought about my mother and how she used to kiss me between my shoulder blades before I went to sleep. Did she know where I was now?"

At 10:25 the braking rockets in the Vostok roared into life and the space capsule began its descent into the earth's atmosphere. "Its outer sheath soon got red-hot," recalled Gagarin. "I could see the sinister crimson reflections of the flame around the module through the curtains covering the portholes. I ceased being weightless and the growing G-loads pushed me into my seat. I was getting nearer the ground all the time."

Four miles above the earth Gagarin felt a sharp jerk. The braking parachute had opened and he began falling more slowly. This was followed by the jettisoning of the hatch door and the landing parachute opened two seconds later.

But the first man in space did not live long to savor that triumph. Seven years later, in 1968, he was killed in a flying accident. Before he died he wrote: "We are children of the earth. To it we owe our lives, warmth and the joy of existing."

The Russians had put a man into space ahead of the Americans—but only 23 days ahead. On the morning of May 5, 1961, U.S. astronaut Alan B. Shepard, Jr. sat in his Mercury spacecraft atop the black and white Redstone booster on its launch pad at Cape Canaveral. At 9:34 A.M. as millions of Americans watched anxiously on their television screens, the rocket ignited and slowly lifted off the pad. At 2.3 seconds after launch, Shepard's voice was heard on radio to Mercury Control "Ah, Roger; lift-off, and the clock is started. Yes, sir, reading you loud and clear. This is Freedom 7. The fuel is go; 1.2G; cabin at 14 psi [pounds per square inch of air pressure]; oxygen is go. Freedom 7 is still go."

Shepard's whole flight lasted only 15 minutes 22 seconds, strictly an up-and-down flight with no orbit, and he was weightless for only about 5 minutes. The Freedom 7 spacecraft rose to an altitude of 116.5 miles, attained a top speed of 5,180 mph, and landed safely 302 miles down range. The test was a complete success.

The United States planned to confirm their findings by Virgil "Gus" Grissom's 16-minute, suborbital mission on July 21. But Grissom's flight nearly ended in tragedy when the explosive escape hatch mechanism accidently blew off while the Liberty Bell 7 spacecraft bobbed in the water awaiting retrieval. Water gushed in. Fortunately, Grissom was able to swim free of the flooding capsule as a hovering helicopter got a line on the floundering spacecraft. The weight of the water-filled capsule was too much for the helicopter, the line was cut, and Grissom's ship sank.

Just 16 days later, on August 6, 1961, the Russians blasted cosmonaut Gherman S. Titov into a 17-orbit, 25-hour 18-minute spaceflight in Vostok 2. The Russians now had more than 26 hours of orbital flight while the United States had yet to put its first astronaut into orbit.

The Mercury-Atlas rocket destined for that task passed its final checkout flight on September 13, carrying a man-sized robot. On November 29, Mercury-Atlas 5 carried Enos, the chimpanzee, on a two-orbit jaunt in space while scientists checked the crucial environmental control system. Then on February 20, 1962, John H. Glenn, Jr. aboard the Friendship 7 spacecraft became the first American to go into orbit. Glenn made 3 orbits in a 4-hour 55-minute flight. Friendship 7's orbit ranged from a high point of 162 miles to a low of 100 miles as Glenn traveled some 83,450 miles at a maximum speed of 17,549 miles per hour.

Glenn experienced about 4 hours and 28 minutes of weightlessness

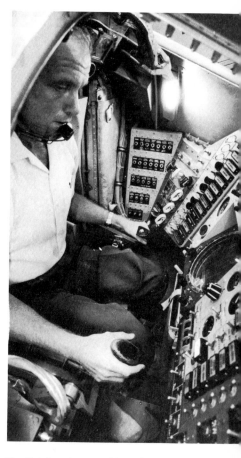

The first American to orbit earth was John Glenn, seen here in his capsule during training. Talking to Congress after his flight in February, 1962, he said, "As our knowledge of this universe increases, may God grant us wisdom and guidance to use it wisely."

"Boy, that was a real fireball." —John Glenn

Lieutenant Colonel John Herschel Glenn, Jr. was lying flat on his back strapped into a form-fit couch in a tiny bubble bristling with instruments. Firmly, in an incredible matter-of-fact voice, he began to count: "Ten, nine, eight, seven, six, five . . ."

Yuri Gagarin's space flight caused jubilation around the world, but in the United States this was tempered with envy. Now they were determined to do better. In May, 1961, Alan B. Shepard, Jr. went into space—but not for an orbit. After climbing 115 miles in Mercury 3, he dropped back into the Atlantic Ocean. Shepard was followed in July by another American, Gus Grissom.

The Russians were back in the space race in August, 1961, when Vostok 2 orbited the earth with cosmonaut Gherman Titov, the first man to eat and sleep in space, and to see the sun rise and set twice in one day.

And now, on the launch pad at Cape Canaveral, it was John Glenn's turn. For three years he had trained for the moment when the giant Atlas-D missile would carry Mercury 6 into orbit.

". . . Zero." A yellow-white gush of flame spewed from the base of the giant missile. For nearly four seconds it seemed as if gravity would triumph. Then, slowly it began to lift toward the brilliant blue sky. "We're under way," reported Glenn.

For the next four hours and 56 minutes John Glenn was to know the meaning of the word miracle. "I don't know what you can say about a day in which you have seen four beautiful sunsets," he said later, "three in orbit, and one after I was back."

There was the wonder of weightlessness, something, reported Glenn, to which he could become addicted. He shook his head violently to see if he would feel sick. Nothing happened. "I have no ill effects from zero G (no gravity)," he reported. "It's very pleasant as a matter of fact. Visual acuity is still excellent. No nausea or discomfort whatsoever." Glenn tested the treat of weightlessness with his camera, after taking pictures through the window. "It seemed perfectly natural; rather than put the camera away, I just put it out in mid-air and let go of it."

Glenn radioed back impressions of his first night in space over the Indian Ocean. The stars were bright diamonds on black velvet. "If you've been out in the desert on a very clear, brilliant night when there's no moon and the stars seem to jump at you, that's just about the way they look."

After crossing the Indian Ocean, John Glenn looked down on the western coast of Australia. He reported that he could see a "big pattern of light, apparently right on the coast." The glow came from thousands of lights in the city of Perth, deliberately turned on by the people of the city to test Glenn's night vision. Streetlights were ablaze, householders turned on their porch lights and spread sheets on the ground as reflectors. When the lights were explained to him, Glenn radioed: "Thank everybody for turning them on, will you?"

Throughout the flight, Glenn reported his impressions. He had little sensation of speed. It was, he said, "about the same as flying in an airliner, at say, 30,000 feet, and looking down at clouds at 10,000 feet." Over California he spotted the irrigated acres around the town of El Centro where he once lived.

But the historic flight of Mercury 6 was not all plain sailing. Instruments reported a loose glass-fibre heat shield which could fall off before or during Glenn's re-entry, killing him in a ball of flame. There was nothing Glenn could do but hope—and as his capsule raced through the atmosphere he watched chunks of metal "as big as the end of your finger to seven or eight inches in diameter" flaming past his window. The nightmare lasted for seven minutes and 15 seconds. Then came Glenn's exultant voice: "Boy, that was a real fireball."

John Glenn had made it. The instruments had been at fault—not the heat shield. The chunks of metal he had seen were disintegrating fragments of the retrorocket. At 2:34 P.M., Mercury 6 hit the waters of the Atlantic with a sizzle as the red-hot shield turned the water to steam. Helicopters from the destroyer *Noa* plucked the capsule out of the water at 3:01—and across the United States television watchers sighed with relief.

Below: a group of cosmonauts during a relaxing break. From left to right, Bykovsky, Tereshkova, Popovich, Nikolayev, and Titov, playing a game of ice hockey in the winter.

Above: the first woman launched into space, Russia's Valentina Tereshkova, underwent the same training as the men before her solo flight on June 16, 1963. She remained the sole woman cosmonaut for 19 years, until her compatriot Svetlana Savitskaya soared into orbit on August 19, 1982.

and a maximum "G-force" of 7.7G's. G-force refers to a magnification of the earth's gravity as the spacecraft accelerates or decelerates on entry or re-entry from space. One G is exactly equal to the force of gravity at the earth's surface. At 1G, a 150-pound man weighs 150 pounds, at 2G's he weighs 300 pounds, at 3G's 450 pounds, and so forth. Scientists were deeply concerned with the effect of the high G-force astronauts would have to experience during their spaceflights. Experiments in giant ground laboratory centrifuges, which produced high G-forces by whirling a man around and around, had indicated that the human body could possibly endure 13G's before losing consciousness. But only a trip into space could answer the question satisfactorily. Gagarin and Glenn had proved that a man could safely endure at least 7.7G's. And that in itself was a major step forward.

After the Glenn flight, America planned an identical flight with another astronaut, M. Scott Carpenter, as pilot. On May 24, Carpenter blasted off for a 3-orbit, 4-hour 56-minute flight. But as the capsule re-entered the atmosphere it failed to orient itself properly and as a result landed some 250 miles off the planned impact point. It took some time for the recovery ship to make radio contact with the floating capsule—for a while an apprehensive nation waited in suspense for word that the astronaut was safe.

On August 11 and 12, 1962, the Russians again demonstrated their growing mastery of manned spaceflight techniques. On the 11th,

cosmonaut Andrian G. Nikolayev blasted off in Vostok 3. The next day, he was joined in space by Vostok 4 piloted by Pavel R. Popovich. The second launching was timed so that on its first orbit Vostok 4 approached within 3.1 miles of its sister ship, achieving the first twin flight of the space age. Popovich stayed up for 48 orbits lasting nearly 71 hours, and Nikolayev set a new 64-orbit, 94-hour 22-minute spaceflight record.

Astronaut Walter M. "Wally" Schirra took off in his Sigma 7 spacecraft on October 3 for a 6-orbit, 9-hour 13-minute flight. The flight, virtually flawless, ended with a splashdown only 5 miles from the target. L. Gordon Cooper, Jr. completed the seventh and last Mercury flight in his Faith 7 spacecraft on May 15, 1963. Cooper's 34-hour and 20-minute stay in space was the first long-duration flight for the Americans. The ground had been laid for "Project Gemini," the next big manned spaceflight series.

Russia, however, continued its manned space research without any let-up. On June 14, 1963, cosmonaut Valery F. Bykovsky aboard Vostok 5 was injected into orbit for a new record manned spaceflight —81 orbits and 119 hours 6 minutes. Two days later, on June 16, the first woman in space, Valentina V. Tereshkova, joined Bykovsky in orbit in Vostok 6. During her 48-orbit, 70-hour and 50-minute flight, Tereshkova passed within 3 miles of Vostok 5 in Vostok 6, again demonstrating the Russian ability for precision launching. This flight

Since each space traveler must be the eyes and ears for earthbound scientists, each return from space is followed by intensive debriefing, so that no detail can be forgotten. Here Russia's Nikolayev reports on his 64-orbit space flight just after his parachute landing.

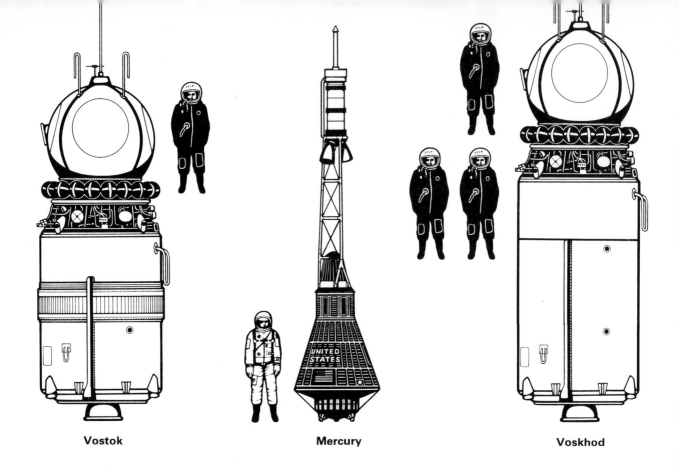

Vostok   **Mercury**   **Voskhod**

was the last of the Vostok series.

A year passed as both nations continued their preparations for more advanced spaceflight. Then on October 12, 1964, the Russians introduced a modified Vostok, known as Voskhod. Cosmonauts Vladimir M. Komarov, Konstantin P. Feoktistov, and Boris P. Egorov flew the first Voskhod through 16 orbits in 24 hours 17 minutes.

The Vostok series and newly introduced Voskhod spacecraft pointed out important differences between the Russian and American approaches to spaceflight. The relatively small Mercury capsules of the American program had been boosted into orbit by the 367,000-pound thrust Mercury-Atlas, a modified ICBM. This "one and a half stage" booster consisted of three engines side by side. The outer engines produced 154,000 pounds of thrust each during liftoff. The central sustainer engine, also ignited at lift-off, generated an additional 57,000 pounds thrust and continued to burn after the two side engines had burned out and dropped off, thus producing the other "half stage." The Atlas had no second stage. The Mercury 3,000-pound capsule was a cone, 9 feet 7 inches from its heat shield to the nose and 6 feet 2 inches at its widest point. It had to be thin-skinned to save precious weight. As a result, the astronaut's life support system could deliver only almost pure oxygen at roughly five pounds per square inch, a third of normal atmospheric pressure. Much thicker walls would have been required to contain full atmospheric pressure—15 pounds per square inch—and these would have added much more weight.

Above: the early Russian and American manned spacecraft: the one-man Mercury flanked by Russia's one-man Vostok and three-man Voskhod. The Vostok spacecraft, in which Gagarin traveled, is almost three times the size of Mercury. This difference meant that the rockets needed to launch the Soviet Union's spacemen into orbit had to be that much more powerful than those needed to send the first American astronauts into space.

Right: these enormously powerful boosters of Russia's Vostok rocket are capable of delivering 1,340,000 pounds of thrust, more than three times that of the Mercury-Atlas rocket which launched America's first astronauts.

The Russians, on the other hand, boosted their Vostoks into orbit with a liquid-fuel ICBM delivering 1,340,000 pounds thrust, more than three times the thrust of the Mercury-Atlas rocket. The main stage consisted of four engines, clustered around a single core engine, which, like the Atlas sustainer engine, burned for a short time after the four strap-ons had burned out and fallen off. The rocket then had a single-engine second stage to accelerate Vostok into orbit.

With so much thrust to work with, the Russians needed far less to be concerned about Vostok's weight than were the Americans who designed the Mercury capsule. The Russian spacecraft was a large sphere with a diameter of $7\frac{1}{2}$ feet. It had heavy solid walls of steel alloy and weighed some 10,400 pounds, or about three and a half times as much as the Mercury capsule. It was divided into two compartments, one for the pilot and one for the equipment. Because of the heavy steel walls, the Russians were able to provide their cosmonauts with an atmosphere similar to the air we breathe—made up of 21 per cent oxygen and the rest mostly nitrogen—at normal atmospheric pressure.

The three-man Voskhod was somewhat heavier than the Vostok—11,731 pounds compared with 10,400—and was designed so that the three cosmonauts sat side by side. The modification was made possible

Cosmonauts Alexei Leonov (top) and Pavel Belyayev aboard their Voskhod 2 spacecraft. During the flight, Leonov crawled out of the spacecraft through an extensible airlock to make the first "walk" in space.

by increasing the thrust of the booster to 1,433,250 pounds, an additional 93,250 pounds. The single-engine second stage was replaced with a new two-engine package. The additional thrust permitted the Russians to increase the weight of Voskhod 2, launched on March 18, 1965 to 12,529 pounds—800 pounds more. The extra weight in Voskhod 2 came from the addition of an airlock, similar to the escape locks on submarines.

Only two cosmonauts flew on the Voskhod 2 mission, Alexei A. Leonov and Pavel I. Belyayev. On this mission, cosmonaut Leonov crawled through the airlock to perform another space "first"—a walk in space. The airlock permitted Leonov to leave the spacecraft and then re-enter it without bringing about a loss of air pressure in the main cosmonaut compartment. For him to leave, the airlock was first pressurized to the level of the main cosmonaut compartment. Leonov crawled into the airlock through a hatch from the main compartment, sealed the hatch, depressurized the airlock, and then opened a second hatch to the outside. His walk in space was really more like an underwater swim. Secured to the spacecraft by a line, he stepped into empty space and floated weightless for about 10 minutes before re-entering the airlock. Once the outside hatch was sealed, the airlock was repressurized and Leonov got back into the main compartment of the spacecraft.

Voskhod 2 and cosmonaut Leonov's spectacular space walk marked the end of a clearly visible division in the space age. Man had entered space. What followed was a new age, a new confidence, and new goals.

Above: a ghostly figure moving outside the spacecraft, Alexei Leonov became the first man to walk in space, while his fellow cosmonaut, Belyayev, kept a watchful eye on him from inside.

Eyes in the Sky
5

For centuries the nomadic Indian people living on the shores of the Gulf of Mexico lived in fear of the great winds that blew in from the sea, bringing death and destruction. Today the hurricanes of the Caribbean still batter the coastal cities of the Gulf—but the inhabitants have time to prepare for the worst.

That vital time is provided by a series of satellites orbiting the earth to give detailed information on changing weather patterns. These satellites—and others like them—now play a key role in the modern world, from communications to navigation, monitoring the spread of nuclear weapons, map-making, agriculture and fishing. About 100 satellites are now launched each year, the majority by the Soviet Union. Over 3,000 satellites have been launched since the space age began, about 3 per cent of which have been manned.

Foremost among the unmanned satellites are communications satellites (comsats), which have fostered a boom in international telephone and TV traffic—and become big business themselves by leasing time to telephone, television and computer users. A satellite

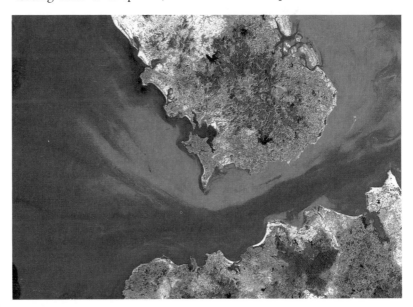

Left: how Gemini 12 saw Arabia, the Red Sea, the United Arab Republic (Egypt), and (center) the Nile Valley, looking south-east. The cloud-like band across the picture is jetstream.

Above: from orbit several hundred miles over China, an earth-resource satellite views the surface with its multi-spectral eyes. By processing the data by computer and applying false colors, images are produced which show a wealth of detail.

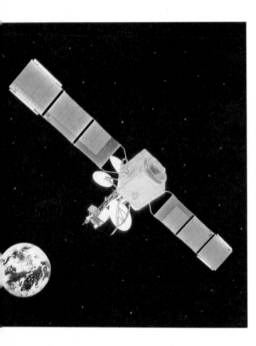

Above: the communications satellite
Intelsat V went into service in the
1980's. A number were launched above
the Atlantic, Pacific and Indian Oceans
for operation into the 1990's. Each is
capable of handling 12,000 telephone
calls at the same time.

Right: an Atlas-Centaur rocket blasts off
the launch pad at Cape Canaveral,
carrying a communications satellite.
This is one of the most powerful and
most reliable of the American heavy
launch vehicles.

allows communications between any number of ground stations. Satellites can carry color TV transmissions, which are beyond the capability of normal telephone cables. And comsats have slashed the cost of international telephone calls.

Several experimental types of satellite were tried—including a shiny balloon called Echo that simply reflected signals beamed at it—before the highly successful Telstar. This satellite, a sphere 32 inches in diameter packed with advanced miniature electronic amplifiers and studded with solar cells to generate electricity from sunlight, was launched by the Americans on July 10, 1962. Two weeks later, it carried the first live TV transmissions from the United States to Europe, inaugurating the era of instant global communications that we now take for granted.

Telstar, and a similar satellite called Relay, orbited earth every three hours or so, which meant that they were not always in sight of any given ground station, and even when they were in sight they had to be tracked as they moved across the sky. Two years later a comsat was put into a much higher orbit, so that it orbited the earth only once every 24 hours. This "geostationary" or "synchronous" orbit means that a satellite in such an orbit over the equator would appear to hang fixed above the earth, allowing uninterrupted communications between ground stations. One satellite is "visible" from about a third of the globe, so that three satellites in geostationary orbit can cover the whole world.

Following this success, an organization known as the International Telecommunication Satellite Corporation (Intelsat) was set up, being a consortium of nations to own and operate a global system of communications satellites. The first Intelsat, the famous Early Bird, could carry 240 telephone conversations or one TV channel.

The latest Intelsat satellites are of enormous dimensions and capacity. The Intelsat VI stands no less than 40 feet high and can handle 30,000 telephone calls at once. The Intelsat satellites also carry a number of TV channels. Other satellites are devoted entirely to carrying TV signals. They can relay programs directly into the home via a small dish antenna.

Second to comsats are the weather satellites which keep a constant watch on clouds and storms around the world, revealing dangerous hurricanes and snow and ice cover, allowing predictions of possible floods caused by melting. Ships receive information about the move-ment of icebergs. Weather satellites have paid for themselves many

Left: computer-enhanced picture of
global weather patterns over Africa,
taken by the European weather
satellite Meteosat.

times by warning of potential hazards. Modern satellites, in addition
to taking photographs, measure the temperature and humidity of the
atmosphere at various levels, as well as the temperature of the land and
sea. Some have been placed in the geostationary orbit, where they can
monitor one face of the earth continuously.

Another, smaller group of satellites scan the earth's crust and
whatever grows upon it and whatever might be found below it. These are
the earth-resource satellites (ERSs), such as the American Landsats and
the French SPOT. By photographing the earth's surface with special
cameras which are sensitive to specific regions of the spectrum, such as
infra-red, ERSs show up vegetation which is diseased, areas of air or
water pollution, and good feeding grounds in the oceans for fish.
Geologists often use ERS pictures to prospect for valuable minerals

Below: a powerful hurricane moves into
the Caribbean from the Atlantic, with
winds blowing in excess of 100 mph.
This picture was taken by a GOES
(Geostationary Operational
Environmental Satellite) in orbit
over the Atlantic Ocean.

Above: one of the Navstar satellites that forms part of the Global Positioning System. This American satellite navigation system comprises 18 Navstar satellites spaced around the globe. They send out signals that enable ships with suitable equipment to determine their position to within about 50 feet.

such as copper ores. Some developing countries have used Landsat pictures to make their first accurate maps.

Throughout history, man has struggled to know his position on earth with ever-increasing accuracy, particularly at sea. Navigation satellites act as artificial guiding stars for navigators at sea or in the air, and for surveyors on earth. The satellites regularly broadcast information on their position in orbit, from which a small computer at the receiving station can work out the navigator's position. Research has led to a network known as the Global Positioning System, available to military and civilian craft, which gives positions within 50 feet or so. Now no one with a suitable receiver need be lost anywhere on earth.

The United States and the Soviet Union use spy satellites to keep an eye on each other's military developments. These satellites are so sophisticated that they can photograph individual vehicles and personnel on the ground. They also make it possible to monitor test-ban treaties and to verify internationally agreed limitations on the spread of nuclear weapons.

Pure science has benefited enormously from astronomy satellites. Early satellites showed that space was more benign than pessimists had feared, and that humans could safely orbit the earth in spacecraft. Satellite-borne telescopes have been able to study distant galaxies, without the interference of the earth's atmosphere. Other satellites have studied the sun, magnetic fields and radiation—particularly x-rays given out by extraordinary energy pulses from outer space. It is this research which has provided strong evidence for the existence of black holes, bizarre objects predicted by theory but never previously known to be real.

A black hole is a part of space where gravity is so strong that nothing can escape, not even light. Black holes are believed to be formed when a dying star collapses at the end of its life. Under the inward pull of its own gravity, the star gets smaller and denser until it finally vanishes from sight into a black hole, leaving an intense gravitational vortex behind it. Although nothing can get out of a black hole, things can get sucked into one like going down a cosmic drainplug. When gas plummets toward a black hole it heats up and emits x-rays before vanishing into oblivion inside the hole, and it is x-rays formed in such a way that satellites are believed to have detected.

Some distant and mysterious objects called quasars are thought to have super-massive black holes at their centers, containing the mass

Above: computer-enhanced picture of
the Baluchistan Desert between Iran
(bottom of picture) and Pakistan (top).
The sand dunes in the top right are
part of Afghanistan. The burnished
colors indicate that the mountains are
rich in metal ores.

Right: this Landsat 4 image shows the
city of Boston and the surrounding
countryside. The processing computer
has chosen false colors so that
vegetation shows up as green, while
urban areas are pink. Note how clearly
the runways of Boston Airport show up.

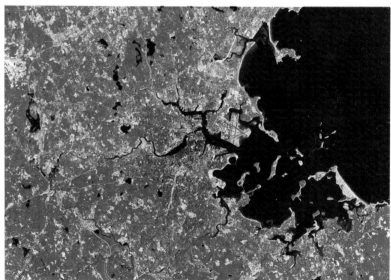

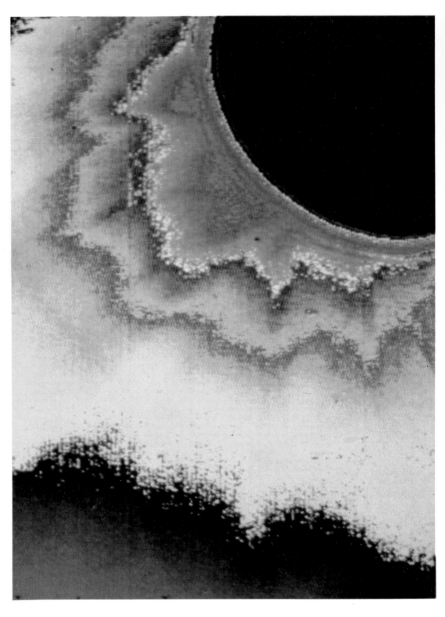

Above: the Hubble space telescope, scheduled for launch from the Space Shuttle in 1990. Because it is located above the earth's distorting atmosphere, it is able to view the universe with unprecedented clarity, seeing stars hundreds of times fainter than we can from earth and up to seven times farther away.

Right: an impression of the sun's corona prepared from data sent back by the NASA Solar Maximum Mission satellite. The colors represent densities of the corona, from blue (densest) to yellow (less dense). The corona has a temperature of about four million degrees Celsius. The blue, dense regions overlie solar sunspot zones.

of millions of stars like the sun. These voracious black holes are believed to swallow up whole stars from space around them, producing a fiery brightness visible clear across the universe. Sure enough, satellites have supported these theories by detecting x-rays coming from the centers of quasars.

Most astronomy satellites carry instruments sensitive to wavelengths that are partly or completely blocked by the earth's atmosphere, such as ultraviolet, x-ray and infra-red. They often give us a totally different view of the universe than we see with light. The Hubble space telescope is the first astronomy satellite to view at optical wavelengths. It carries a 94-inch diameter mirror to collect the light. Launched by the Space Shuttle, it is also designed to be serviced periodically by Shuttle astronauts.

Unmanned satellites and what they do

TYPE OF SATELLITE	DESCRIPTION
Communications satellites	These relay telephone, telex, and TV signals between ground stations around the world. Telstar, launched in July, 1962, carried the first live transatlantic TV transmissions. Syncom 3, in August, 1964, was the first communications satellite in geostationary orbit. The world is now linked by satellites in the internationally owned and operated Intelsat series. Several countries have their own satellites for domestic communications.
Weather satellites	These observe the earth's atmosphere and clouds, allowing meteorologists to make more accurate forecasts and for longer in advance. The United States Tiros 1, in April, 1960, was the first weather satellite. The world's weather is now kept under constant watch by satellites of various nations.
Earth resources (remote sensing) satellites	Satellites such as the United States Landsat series observe the earth's surface and oceans, providing information to geologists that helps them prospect for minerals and study the earth's landforms and land usage. Special cameras follow the growth of crops and other vegetation, and monitor the spread of pollution in the sea and air. Radar is used to study ocean waves and the nature of soils.
Navigation satellites	These broadcast regular signals from orbit which allow navigators to fix their positions anywhere on the globe with greater precision than other methods. The United States Navy's Transit 1, launched on April 13, 1960, was the first navigation satellite.
Spy satellites	These photograph military forces and missile emplacements, eavesdrop on military communications, and monitor nuclear explosions. They are vital for monitoring observance of test-ban treaties and arms limitations agreements.
Astronomy satellites	These observe the universe at a variety of wavelengths from gamma-ray to infra-red. The United States launched some of the first astronomical satellites, called Orbiting Astronomical Observatories. Other satellites have included the British Ariel V, which looked for x-ray emissions from black holes; the International Ultraviolet Explorer, a Joint American-European venture; the Solar Maximum Mission; and IRAS, the infra-red astronomy satellite, which spotted stars being born.

Rehearsing for the Moon
6

In order to practice working in the weightless conditions of space, scientists have simulated space conditions here on earth. Here Edwin Aldrin experiences weightlessness floating in an underwater test chamber.

From 1961 to 1965, the objectives of both the Russian and the American space programs had been to learn how to get into space; and once there, probing slowly and cautiously, to find out whether man might live in space and, if so, how. By the end of the Mercury program the United States had gained sufficient experience in launching men into space to have some confidence in its rocket boosters, its worldwide tracking network, and its recovery procedures. The Russians had shown that a man could actually survive outside his space capsule. Early fears about the ill effects of prolonged weightlessness in space were dispelled. Some problems had appeared, but they were not insurmountable. The manned spaceflights already achieved had proved that man could pilot a spacecraft himself. Apart from controlling the spacecraft when necessary, the astronaut or cosmonaut could perform scientific tasks, take photographs, and even walk outside the space capsule. The two space nations could now start thinking about what they wanted to do next.

The Russians were secretive. Little is known, even today, about what their intentions really were. They would announce the results of successful space missions, but would not enlarge on or explain them. The United States, on the other hand, had clearly stated its goal: on May 25, 1961, President John F. Kennedy, in a special message to Congress, made the following declaration: "I believe this nation should commit itself to achieving the goal, before this decade is out, of landing a man on the moon and returning him safely to the earth. No single space project in this period will be more impressive to mankind, or more important for the long-range exploration of space; and none will be so difficult or expensive to accomplish." From that moment on, the space race had become the moon race.

Project Gemini, the second American series of manned spaceflights, was conceived to develop and practice the techniques required for a lunar landing mission. The two-man Gemini capsule was far more sophisticated than its Mercury counterpart. It consisted of a re-entry module in which the crew returned to earth, and an adapter module. The adapter unit contained retrorockets to begin re-entry, fuel tanks, and fuel cells to supply electricity. It was jettisoned just before re-entry into the atmosphere began. The re-entry module—also known as the crew capsule—contained, in addition to the crew, radios and radar, flight controls, the life support systems, and a small computer to assist in maneuvering. The re-entry and adapter modules, which made up the whole of the orbiting spacecraft, together weighed more than

7,000 pounds, more than twice the weight of the Mercury capsule.

The Gemini spacecraft was to be boosted into orbit by the Gemini-Titan 2. This two-stage rocket stood 103 feet high and had a 10-foot diameter. Its dual chamber first-stage engine developed a 430,000-pound thrust at liftoff. The second stage delivered another 100,000-pound thrust for orbit.

The combination Gemini spacecraft and Titan 1 rocket—without a passenger—made its first successful test flight in April, 1964. The second and last unmanned test flight, Gemini-Titan 2, took place in January, 1965. Project Gemini was ready to go.

A space voyage to the moon and back takes about eight days. The Russians had collected medical information during cosmonaut Valery Bykovsky's five-day stint in Vostok 5, but what they knew was not available to the United States. The longest flight by an American astronaut had been Gordon Cooper's 34-hour flight in Mercury 9. Cooper's flight and other Mercury missions had raised some medical questions that worried the aerospace physicians. Most of the problems seemed to result from the prolonged weightlessness experienced in spaceflight. One troubling feature was that as the astronauts' hearts relaxed—because they did not have to work against gravity—blood pooled in their legs and feet causing painful swellings. Passengers on long-distance buses experience a similar effect after several hours spent sitting in the same position. There were also indications that the astronauts' muscles lost tone, and that during long missions their bones lost mineral content and tended to become soft. The doctors thought that the difficulties might be overcome by a program of exercises to be carried out within the capsule and by redesigning the pressurized spacesuits to be worn by astronauts during flights. However, this was still theory.

There were other problems to be solved, besides keeping the astronauts fit, before a lunar landing team could be launched. On a long flight beyond the earth, the astronauts might be called on to make emergency repairs on the outside of their spacecraft. In theory, experts knew, a man should be able to crawl out of the capsule and work in space. But this had never been tested—and difficulties might arise. The Gemini mission was to answer these questions.

Getting a man on the moon and off again called for complicated and still untested maneuvers in space. The lunar-orbit rendezvous method would require a precision maneuver in lunar orbits so that the lunar module (LM) could reunite with the command module after blasting

Left: this photograph was taken from Gemini 6 as Gemini 7 was about to complete the first rendezvous in space. The two craft were about 9 feet apart at this point.

off from the moon's surface. There were two parts to this vital operation—the rendezvous, or meeting in orbit, and then the even more delicate docking of the two spacecraft. This crucial maneuver would require extensive practice.

First, however, the Gemini spacecraft had to be checked out in manned flight. The job fell to Mercury veteran Gus Grissom, and to astronaut John W. Young, going up for the first time. On March 23, 1965, five days after Alexei Leonov's historic "spacewalk" from Voskhod 2, Gemini 3 blasted off for a perfect three-orbit, 5-hour mission. During the flight, Grissom and Young successfully tested the spacecraft's maneuvering ability. They moved it up and down and sideways, and even changed the orbit. The Gemini proved flightworthy.

On June 3, Gemini 4 made 62 orbits in a little under 98 hours. Command pilot James A. McDivitt handled the controls while astronaut Edward H. White took a 21-minute space walk outside the spacecraft. Attached to the spacecraft by a 50-foot "umbilical cord," White maneuvered around in empty space using a hand-held, gasfiring jet gun. He had a wonderful time snapping pictures and joking with McDivitt, enjoying it all so much that McDivitt finally had to plead with him to return to the spacecraft. Gemini 4 was noteworthy, too,

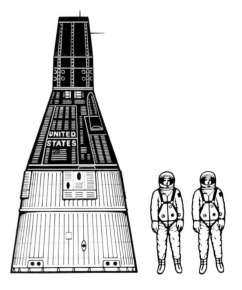

Although the Gemini capsule was small it answered many questions about man's ability to survive in space.

75

Astronauts Grissom and Young being sealed into Gemini 3. During their five-hour flight in earth orbit they tested the spacecraft's maneuvering ability and general flightworthiness.

Above: Stafford and Cernan about to enter Gemini 9, in which they proved the versatility and reliability of the space capsule. But due to technical difficulties they could not perform the delicate docking maneuver in space.

because it was the first flight to be controlled from the multimillion dollar Mission Control at the Manned Spacecraft Center near Houston, Texas. This flight began the vital training of some 600 technicians who would monitor and control all the future manned flights including the lunar mission.

Gemini 5's primary mission, begun on August 21, was to test how men, in the tiny spacecraft, stood up to eight full days of confinement—the estimated time for the moon mission. Astronauts L. Gordon Cooper, Jr. and Charles "Pete" Conrad, Jr. quickly discovered that on this occasion they had more than prolonged weightlessness to contend with. The new electricity-producing fuel cell, carried by Gemini 5 in place of batteries because it was smaller and lighter in weight, started losing pressure. This lowered its electricity output and threatened to shut down some of the spacecraft's control systems. Mission Control considered the situation serious, possibly serious enough to mean an early end to the mission and thus a failure in the primary goal. Astronauts Cooper and Conrad, however, rationed their electrical consumption to absolute needs and nursed the faulty fuel cell through the full eight days.

Thorough medical examination of the two astronauts after the mission showed that they were in perfect health and had apparently suffered no serious or lasting effects from the flight—man's longest in space thus far.

The next major hurdle was the difficult rendezvous and docking maneuver. This mission was assigned to Gemini 6. According to the flight plan, an Agena rocket would first be placed into orbit, and then the Gemini 6 spacecraft would be launched to attempt a rendezvous and docking with the orbiting rocket. But things did not work out that way. On October 25, 1965, as astronauts Walter M. Schirra, Jr. and Thomas P. Stafford waited in their spacecraft atop their booster, the target vehicle lifted cleanly off its launch pad and rose through the atmosphere. Then, just before attaining orbit, it exploded. With no target to chase, the disappointed astronauts climbed back out of their spacecraft and had dinner at home.

The Gemini 7 mission, scheduled for December, was to be a 14-day test of man's ability to survive in space. After the Gemini 6 failure, NASA officials decided to double up the two missions. Gemini 7 would be launched as planned, and then Gemini 6 would be lifted into orbit to rendezvous with it. On December 4, astronauts Frank Borman and James A. Lovell, Jr. blasted off in Gemini 7 for their 2-week stay in orbit. Gemini 6 was scheduled to follow on December 12. But at the moment of ignition, an electrical connection feeding the booster became loose. The rocket shut down with Schirra and Stafford still sitting in their spacecraft. Three days later, however, a third launch attempt succeeded, and Gemini 6 was on its way.

Once in orbit, Schirra, a space veteran, chased Gemini 7 for over 100,000 miles at a speed of more than 17,000 miles per hour. He caught his quarry at an altitude of 185 miles and drew within one foot of it, having successfully achieved man's first rendezvous in space. The two Gemini ships then flew in formation for several hours. Finally, Gemini 6 moved away from the other spacecraft, fired its retrorockets, and returned to earth. Gemini 7 then completed its 2-week, 206-orbit mission and the two astronauts were recovered in perfect health.

Floating several hundred miles above the Pacific Ocean, on the end of a thin tether, Edwin Aldrin proved it was possible for man to do useful tasks in space.

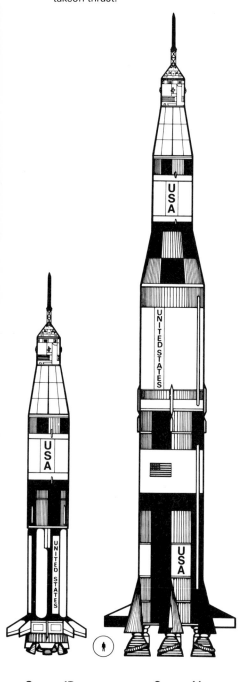

Below: before the Apollo lunar series could begin, the Saturn IB had to be developed to carry a far greater payload Saturn V stands 140 feet taller than its forerunner with five times as much takeoff thrust.

Saturn IB   **Saturn V**

On March 16, 1966, Gemini 8 achieved a full rendezvous and docking with a rocket already in orbit. The mission had its tense moments. Only hours after astronauts Neil A. Armstrong and David R. Scott blasted off their launch pad, Armstrong successfully completed the docking. Then, while still docked, the spacecraft began spinning wildly when a thruster rocket stuck open. After less than 11 hours in space, Mission Control cut the flight short and ordered Gemini 8 to make an emergency splashdown in the Pacific.

Gemini 9, with astronauts Tom Stafford and Eugene A. Cernan aboard, also had problems. Its primary goal was another practice rendezvous and docking. But this time the protective metal shroud over the target rocket's docking collar was not blown completely off by the explosives. Stafford said the half-opened, clamshell-like shroud looked "like an angry alligator." Docking was out of the question, but Stafford did guide his spacecraft to three different rendezvous positions and Cernan took a long space walk to test man's ability to perform simple tasks outside the spacecraft. After 72 hours 21 minutes in space Gemini 9 demonstrated its ability to be "flown" down to a precision landing. Then on July 18, John Young and Michael Collins took off in Gemini 10 for another 3-day rendezvous and docking mission. They rendezvoused with their own target and the still-orbiting Gemini 8 target. After docking with their own target, they retrieved an instrument-package from it and returned to earth, their mission successfully completed.

On September 12, Charles Conrad, Jr. and Richard F. Gordon, Jr. rendezvoused and docked their Gemini 11 spacecraft with yet another target rocket, then refired its engine. The two joined vehicles roared 850 miles out into space before returning. It was the farthest man had ever been from earth. Gemini 12, the final mission of the series, blasted off on November 11. Pilot James A. Lovell, Jr. carried out another successful docking. After that Edwin E. Aldrin took three spacewalks, and, in a total of 5½ hours outside the spaceship he proved that it was possible for a human being to perform a number of useful tasks while in space. After 59 orbits in almost 4 days, Gemini 12 returned to earth, bringing the Gemini series to an end.

Despite the occasional mishaps, Project Gemini had been extremely successful. It had demonstrated man's ability to withstand prolonged weightlessness and his ability to work in space outside his spacecraft, and it had provided vital practice in rendezvous and docking.

While the Gemini series represented the most visible and dramatic part of the preparation for the moon mission, three equally important major projects were under way at the same time. First and foremost was the design and construction of the Apollo spacecraft which combined three separate units: the command module, the service module, and the lunar module. To lift all this into orbit and send it off to the moon required the building of the mammoth Saturn V booster, and the vast "moonport" on Merritt Island at Cape Canaveral.

The Saturn rocket program really began in 1957, long before "Project Apollo" was put on the planning boards. Saturn I was the first member of the family, followed by the Saturn IB. Both incorporated eight engines in their first stage. Saturn IB had a take-off thrust of 1.6 million pounds.

The early Saturns were powerful, but the moon rocket, Saturn V, was very much more powerful—the most powerful rocket yet built. Its first stage was a cluster of five engines, each generating as much as the entire Saturn I, to give a total of 7.5 million pounds thrust. Its second stage consisted of five engines, generating a total thrust of 1 million pounds. The third stage made use of the second stage Saturn IB engine, generating 200,000 pounds thrust.

Everything about the Saturn V was gigantic. Topped with the Apollo spacecraft, the vehicle stood 363 feet high and weighed nearly

The assembled Saturn V rocket was carried over three miles to the launching pad, on a flat rectangular crawler-transporter, driven by eight giant tractors. The slow trip took almost eight hours.

The huge Saturn V rocket was assembled in the Vehicle Assembly Building that stands 525 feet high and was built especially for the rockets needed for lunar exploration.

3,000 tons fully fueled. At liftoff, it used 900 tons of fuel a minute. It could put 120 tons of payload into orbit or send 45 tons to the moon.

Final assembly of the Saturn Vs took place at the moonport on Merritt Island, just inland from Cape Canaveral, about 3½ miles from the launch pad. They were put together in the gigantic Vehicle Assembly Building (VAB), so large that clouds and rain would develop inside it if it were not air-conditioned. The building stands 525 feet high and contains 130 million cubic feet of space (it is now used for assembly of Space Shuttle vehicles).

The Apollo mooncraft itself consisted of three separate modules. The 5-ton command module was cone-shaped like the Mercury and Gemini capsules. It stood 12½ feet high and was 13 feet in diameter at its base. It was the only portion that returned to earth.

Directly behind the command module was the 25-ton service module which contained oxygen supplies for the astronauts, fuel cells for electricity, communications equipment, and a system of small thrusters for maneuvering during rendezvous and docking. From the astronauts' point of view the most important part of the service module was the large main rocket engine that put Apollo into lunar orbit and then propelled it back to earth. Immediately before re-entry the service module was jettisoned and burned up like a meteor as it plunged into the earth's atmosphere.

The third component of the mooncraft was the lunar module (LM). At launch this was stowed below the service module in the top stage of the Saturn rocket. Once on the way to the moon, the command and service modules were turned to dock with the lunar module and extract it from the spent third stage, which was then jettisoned.

The astronauts could crawl through a tunnel in the command module's nose to get into the LM. In orbit around the moon, two astronauts entered the LM and descended in it toward the surface under control of the LM's main landing engine. The LM touched down on its four spiderlike legs. When their exploration of the lunar surface was over, the astronauts took off again in the upper stage of the LM, using the lower half as a launch pad. After docking with the Apollo mother ship circling overhead, the astronauts rejoined their colleague inside, and jettisoned the LM before heading back to earth.

Work on the Apollo spacecraft began in 1962. It was ready for flight

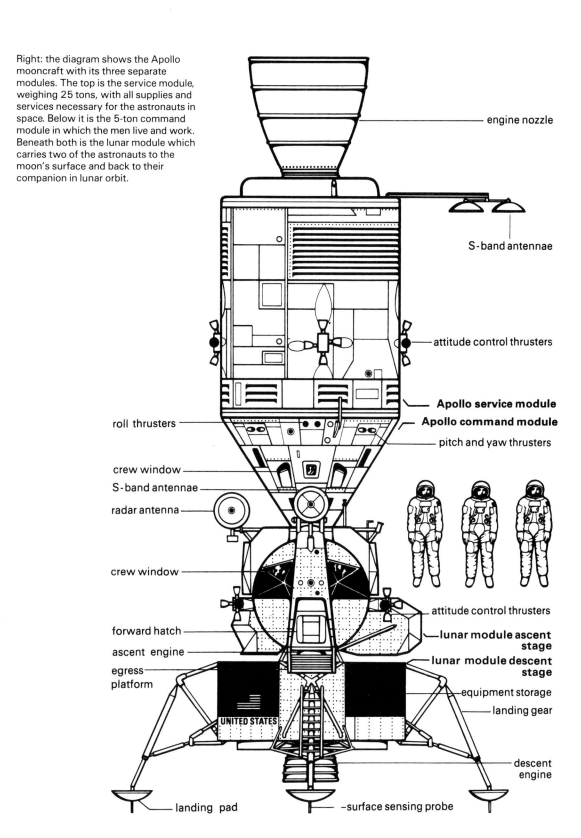

Right: the diagram shows the Apollo mooncraft with its three separate modules. The top is the service module, weighing 25 tons, with all supplies and services necessary for the astronauts in space. Below it is the 5-ton command module in which the men live and work. Beneath both is the lunar module which carries two of the astronauts to the moon's surface and back to their companion in lunar orbit.

engine nozzle

S-band antennae

attitude control thrusters

Apollo service module

Apollo command module

roll thrusters

pitch and yaw thrusters

crew window

S-band antennae

radar antenna

crew window

attitude control thrusters

lunar module ascent stage

forward hatch

ascent engine

lunar module descent stage

egress platform

equipment storage

landing gear

UNITED STATES

descent engine

landing pad

surface sensing probe

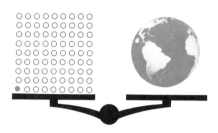

Above: we know that the moon has only 1/81 the weight of the earth. This means that if the earth were placed on a pair of scales, it would take 81 moons to bring the scales to a balance.

Below: this drawing of the moon by Galileo shows the amazing amount of detail he observed with his crude telescope. He discovered that the moon was not a smooth sphere as believed but was marked with valleys and mountains.

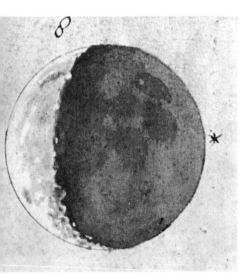

testing in 1967. But 1967 was to prove a disastrous year for both American and Soviet plans to reach the moon. As the Apollo engineers and astronauts struggled with the problems of the moon launch, other scientists pondered the questions about what men would find when they finally got to the moon. There was urgency to these questions because the lives of the astronauts depended, to a certain extent, on the ability of the Apollo planners to make correct assumptions. For example, if they were wrong in assuming the lunar crust could support the weight of the LM the result might be tragedy.

At the beginning of the space age, all that was known about the moon was what could be seen through telescopes from the ground or what astronomers could calculate on the basis of known physical laws.

It is known that the moon's diameter is 2,160 miles, about one-fourth that of the earth, and that its mass is 81 times less than that of the earth. The moon, the earth's only natural satellite, revolves around the earth in not quite a circular orbit once every 27 days, 7 hours, and 43 minutes, and rotates on its axis once during each revolution, with the end result that the same side of the moon always faces the earth. Scientists were able to compute that the moon's gravity at its surface would be about one-sixth that of the earth's. Earth-based instruments were able to detect no indication of an atmosphere. It was thought that if the moon once had an atmosphere, the weakness of its gravity had been unable to hold it. Without the temperature-moderating effects of an atmosphere, it was calculated that temperatures at the lunar surface ranged from a day-time high of about 250°F to a night-time low of 280°F below zero.

Direct telescopic observations of the lunar landscape showed rugged highlands and ridges of high, craggy mountains. These were interspersed with mysterious dark, seemingly flat plains that earlier astronomers had mistaken for seas. These dark flat areas were named *maria*, the plural of the Latin word *mare* for sea. Much of the lunar surface is heavily pocked with craters resulting from the interminable pounding from large and small meteoroids raining in from interplanetary space. (Only the largest meteoroids reach the earth's surface as meteorites, as the smaller ones are burned up by friction in their flight through the atmosphere.) Great cracks, faults, and deep valleys are also visible through some of the more powerful earth-based telescopes.

Two other features of the lunar surface are less easy to explain. The first, streaks of light-colored material, called rays, radiate outward for hundreds of miles from some lunar craters. These rays were believed

Right: soon after its invention, the telescope was used all over Europe. This painting by Donato Creti, in about 1700, shows two astronomers using a Galilean telescope to observe the moon.

Below: a replica of the telescope that Galileo used in his researches. The instrument was capable of magnifying an object 30 times. The invention of the telescope in 1608 opened the way for the development of astronomy.

to be debris thrown out as giant meteoroids smashed into the surface to create the craters. Then, even more mysterious, are the sinuous, meandering lines, called rilles, that look strikingly like the dried river-beds found on earth. In fact, they were probably formed by rivers of hot molten lava escaping from the interior of the moon.

Astronomers also wanted to find out more about how the moon formed. One of a number of hypotheses about the moon's origins suggested that the moon evolved separately from the earth, perhaps as a small planet, and was captured by the earth's gravitational field to become a satellite. Another hypothesis was based on the idea that the moon was torn off the earth during an early period in the planet's formation. Some scientists have gone so far as to pinpoint the Pacific Ocean basin as the place from which the moon was torn. Others said that the moon and earth were formed side by side, just as we see them today. The Apollo missions did not conclusively answer the question of the moon's origin, but most astronomers now prefer the side-by-side theory.

Then, there is the question of whether original moon material was hot or cold. Most experts now believe that the moon (like the earth) was originally hot. If this were so, it would hold the key to understanding the features now visible on the moon, particularly the maria. Many scientists believe that the maria were formed from vast lava flows. Some think that lunar volcanoes spewed the lava forth from a hot interior as

The very first space rocket launched toward the moon was the Russian Luna 1 in 1959, the last stage of which is seen here. But the probe missed the moon and became the first man-made object to orbit around the sun.

earth volcanoes do here. Others maintain the interior of the moon was always cold and suggest that the lava might have been formed when giant meteoroids crashed into the moon, melting large quantities of rock by the sheer force of their impact. This molten rock filled in depressions in the lunar crust and solidified again into the smooth, broad masses that are called the maria.

In terms of Project Apollo, the most frightening of the theories about the maria was that they were not lava beds at all, but vast fields of fine dust accumulated through a thousand million year shower of micrometeoroids. If this were so, then the dust might be many hundreds of feet deep. And a spacecraft, even a small one, could sink in the dust and be swallowed up as if it had landed in quicksand.

At the beginning of the space age, too many important questions about the moon's surface were unanswered. It would have been foolhardy to attempt a manned lunar mission without additional information. For this reason, both the United States and the Soviet Union instituted several series of unmanned probes into the vicinity of the moon and directly to the lunar surface.

The Soviet Union led the way in the unmanned exploration of the moon just as it had with the first earth satellite and the first man in space. On January 2, 1959, the Russians launched their 3,245-pound

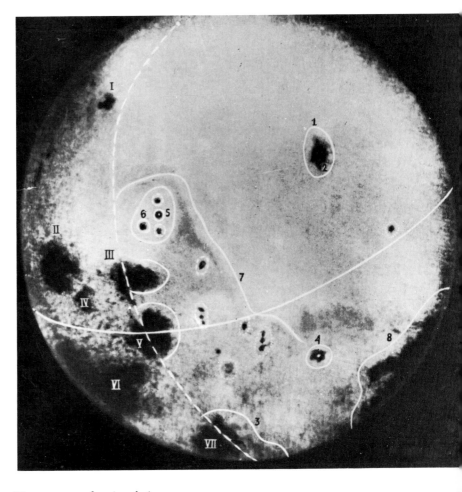

First picture of the far side of the moon, sent back by Luna 3. The continuous line indicates the lunar equator and the broken line the border between the area visible from the earth and the back of the moon. The numbers show the major landmarks.

1. The Sea of Moscow, a large crater sea 300 kms. in diameter
2. The Gulf of Astronauts
3. The continuation of the Southern Sea on the far side of the moon
4. Tsiolkovsky Crater
5. Lomonosov Crater
6. Joliot-Curie Crater
7. Sovietsky Mountain Range
8. The Sea of Dreams

I. Humboldt Sea
II. The Sea of Crises
III. The Marginal Sea
IV. The Sea of Waves
V. Smythe Sea
VI. The Sea of Fertility
VII. The Southern Sea

Luna 1 spacecraft toward the moon. The spacecraft missed the moon, but instead became the first man-made object to go into orbit around the sun.

Luna 2 was more successful. It crashed on the lunar surface on September 13, 1959, to become the first man-made object on the moon. Then, three weeks later, on October 4, the second anniversary of Sputnik 1, Luna 3 circled around the moon and sent back the first pictures of the back of the moon. Although crude by later standards, they created a sensation at the time. The side that always faces away from the earth turned out to be as barren and crater-pocked as the long-familiar front of the moon.

The United States suffered 15 successive failures with moon probes, first with nine Pioneers and then with six of the early Ranger spacecraft. The 807-pound Rangers, each carrying six TV cameras, were designed to crash onto the moon, relaying pictures of the surface back to earth during the last 20 minutes before impact. Ranger 6, in January 1964, hit the moon but sent back no pictures.

Finally, on July 28, 1964, Ranger 7 was launched and sent back 4,316 pictures of the Sea of Clouds before crashing. During 1965, Rangers 8 and 9 were equally successful in photographing the Sea of Tranquility and a highland area near the Sea of Clouds. The Ranger pictures

The United States' Ranger series of lunar spacecraft were designed to transmit information back to earth. This information was then studied by scientists working on man's first flight to the moon. Ranger 7, seen here, was launched in July, 1964, and transmitted nearly 4,500 pictures of the Sea of Clouds before it crashed onto the surface of the moon. A soft landing on the moon was not accomplished for almost another 2 years.

showed details up to 1,000 times smaller than visible from earth. They showed small craters and rocks, some only 10 inches wide. It looked as if there were some areas on the lunar surface smooth enough for a spacecraft landing. There were fewer loose rocks and boulders than scientists expected, but the major scientific questions as to the dust covering and whether the lunar surface could support the weight of a manned spacecraft remained unanswered.

After the Ranger series, the United States concentrated its efforts on two other unmanned lunar programs, Surveyor and Orbiter. While the hardware for these two efforts was still under development, the Soviet Union attempted to soft-land an instrument-package on the moon. The circular, 220-pound Russian instrument-package contained batteries, a

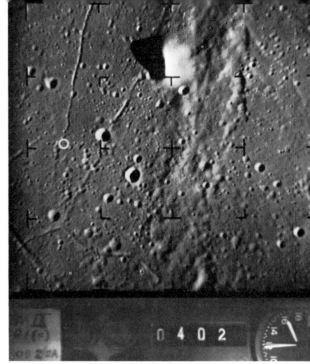

These photographs are two chosen from the several thousands taken by Ranger 9 and transmitted back to the earth. They show the lunar surface in considerably more detail than it had been seen before. Although these pictures were helpful in answering a large number of the scientists' queries, they still left the major question concerning the structure of the moon's crust to be answered.

television camera, and communications equipment. The package was to be carried to the moon by a larger spacecraft and then gently dropped on the surface just before the larger vehicle crashed. On the first five attempts the whole works crashed. But on February 3, 1966, Luna 9 delivered its ball-like instrument-package safely onto the lunar surface. After the package came to rest, petal-like protective panels fell away and the camera switched itself on. Luna 9 sent back 27 close-up pictures before its batteries died.

On April 3, the 540-pound Luna 10, carrying instruments to measure the moon's radiation and magnetism, became the first spacecraft to go into an orbit around the moon. Data from Luna 10 indicated that the moon's crust might be composed of basaltic rock, similar to that in the earth's crust.

For the Americans, success came first time with their Surveyor soft-landing probes, which were designed to fire retrorockets as they approached the lunar surface. On June 2, 1966, Surveyor 1 gently set down on the moon's Ocean of Storms and proceeded to transmit 11,237 pictures of the moon's surface before being shut down six weeks later. Surveyor 2 crashed, but on April 20, 1967, Surveyor 3 landed on the Ocean of Storms and not only sent back pictures but also, in response to command signals from ground control on earth, dug a small trench in the surface with a metal claw. Pictures of the operation showed that the lunar soil was a clumpy, fine-grained stuff that did not appear to offer any problems to future astronauts.

Surveyor 4 failed, but Surveyor 5 arrived safely at the Sea of Tranquility on September 11, 1967. This Surveyor carried an equipment box to analyse the composition of the lunar soil. The data radioed back by Surveyor 5 indicated that, at least in the spot where it had landed, the rocks appeared to be similar to volcanic basalt rock on earth.

Surveyor 6 landed on the moon's Central Bay on November 10,

Above: the moon's crust, a picture by Surveyor. This was part of the first series of color pictures from the moon.

Left: the Surveyor 3 spacecraft performed a series of complicated operations following a perfect soft landing on the Ocean of Storms.

sending back more pictures and soil analysis. The last of the Surveyors, Surveyor 7, landed in a highland area near to the crater Tycho Brahe on January 10, 1968.

The Lunar Orbiters were the final unmanned lunar spacecraft series preparatory to Project Apollo. The series began on August 10, 1966, and ended a year later. All five Lunar Orbiter spacecraft were successful. The first three Orbiters, launched in August and November of 1966 and February, 1967, circled at the moon's equator, carefully photographing what were considered the five most promising landing sites for the first Apollo mission. These three were so successful that it

was decided to place the last two Orbiters, launched in May and August of 1967, in polar orbits. This allowed them to photograph 99 per cent of the moon's surface as it rotated under them.

Their most intriguing discovery, however, was made from an analysis of their motion in orbit around the moon which showed several curious dips. Scientists concluded that these dips could be caused only by large masses of heavy material buried beneath the lunar surface and exerting a slightly stronger gravitational attraction than the rest of the surface. They called these "mascons"—a contraction of mass concentrations. The five main mascons appeared to be located under the five circular lunar seas: Maria Imbrium, Serenitatis, Crisium, Nectaris, and Humorum. Scientists eventually concluded that the mascons were caused by dense rock that had solidified under the maria.

All this space probe activity meant that the moon was quite well known by the time the first astronauts arrived there in 1969. While Apollo astronauts roamed the lunar surface, the Soviet Union showed considerable ingenuity in exploring the moon by unmanned probes. On September 20, 1970, the robot probe Luna 16 touched down on the moon's Sea of Fertility and scooped up a handful of soil before blasting off back to the earth. The amount of moon soil returned was 3½ ounces, paltry compared with the 120 pounds of carefully documented samples already collected by Apollos 11 and 12, but it helped extend scientists' knowledge of the lunar surface. Luna 20 in February, 1972, and Luna 24 in August, 1976, repeated the operation at other sites.

Above: the eight-wheeled Lunokhod 1 moon-roving vehicle, which landed on the moon in November, 1970. Soviet ground controllers steered it by remote control from earth, viewing the lunar surface with TV eyes. It covered 6½ miles during its 10-month lifetime. An improved Lunokhod 2 followed in January, 1973.

The Final Preparations

7

By the end of 1966, preparations for Project Apollo were well advanced. The command and service modules had been tested in unmanned flight around the earth, launched by Saturn IB, the smaller of the two Saturn rockets. The next step was a manned flight of Apollo in earth orbit, to be called Apollo 4. But there was tragedy ahead.

On January 27, 1967, the three astronauts of Apollo 4 were going through a dummy countdown on the launch pad. Veteran astronaut Gus Grissom was in command. His crew were Edward H. White, the first American to walk in space, and Roger B. Chaffee, a naval officer going up for the first time. At 6 P.M. the astronauts, who had been strapped in their couches since shortly after noon, were working their way through the countdown just as if it were the real thing. Even the cabin had been pressurized with the 100 per cent oxygen atmosphere required by American spaceship design. The IB Saturn rocket contained no fuel, so there were no fire crews or doctors standing by.

Suddenly—at exactly 6:31:03 P.M.—a frantic voice came over the intercom, "Fire—I smell fire!" Instruments in the blockhouse showed signs of movement in the spacecraft as the astronauts began groping to force open the sealed hatch. "Fire in the cockpit!" Colonel White was heard to cry. Instruments showed that the cabin temperature was rising sharply. "There's a bad fire in the cockpit," one astronaut shouted. Then came sounds of unintelligible shouting and frantic movement as the astronauts clawed and pounded on the hatch. A last cry of distress from Chaffee: "We're on fire—get us out of here!"

Investigators now believe that a faulty wire near Grissom's couch on the left side of the cockpit sparked off the fire. In the 100 per cent oxygen atmosphere, normally fire-resistant materials easily burst into flame. The spark probably ignited a nylon netting strung under the couches during the test to prevent objects from falling into the equipment area below. The burning nylon in turn carried the flame to other parts of the cabin. In seconds, the oxygen-fed fire turned the command module into a blast furnace.

Within just 14 seconds from the first spark the heat raised the cabin pressure to 29 pounds per square inch, twice as high as normal. The walls of the cabin ruptured at that point and the fire began to smolder in a thick black smoke. The investigating board said the cabin atmosphere must have become lethal 24 seconds after the fire began. The astronauts had lost consciousness within 15 to 30 seconds after the fire started. They died from smoke inhalation, the first fatalities of the space age.

Left: having completed their independent flight in the lunar module, astronauts James McDivitt and Russell Schweickart rejoined the LM to the command module before David Scott stepped into space, the second man on the Apollo 9 flight to do so.

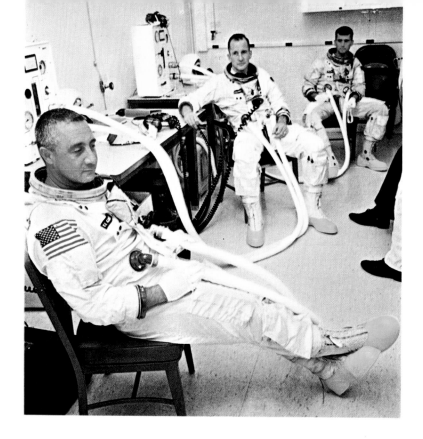

Above: astronauts Grissom, White, and Chaffee were named as the crew for Apollo 4, and from that time on they trained together as a team. They were together one day in January, 1967, rehearsing the launch in the Apollo capsule when a sudden fire broke out.

Above right: the fire killed the three men within seconds, charring the capsule. A stunned nation was faced with the first fatalities of the space program.

The investigating board spelled out the deficiencies: loose, shoddy wiring, excessive use of combustible materials in spite of the obvious fire hazard of a 100 per cent oxygen atmosphere, inadequate provision for emergency rescue, and a three-layer escape hatch that could not be opened in less than 90 seconds under any circumstances. The astronauts had not had a chance.

Project Apollo ground to a halt while the design deficiencies were put right. Flammable materials were replaced with others more fire-resistant. A new fire-resistant spacesuit was ordered. A quick-opening escape hatch was designed. And the spacecraft was put through extensive fire tests in the laboratories.

Plans were laid for a new flight. Mercury and Gemini veteran Wally Schirra was named to command, astronauts Donn F. Eisele and R. Walter Cunningham were his crew.

Even as the United States was grieving over its space martyrs, tragedy also struck the Soviet Union. On April 23, 1967, Vladimir Komarov soared into the heavens on board a new spacecraft, called Soyuz (meaning union). He was hurriedly recalled on his 18th orbit, and successfully negotiated re-entry. But afterwards he was killed when the main braking parachute failed to deploy properly.

Project Apollo slowly returned to life. By October, 1968, all was ready for Apollo 7. In the 21 months since the three astronauts had died the space capsule had been redesigned. The service module had proved itself and the big Saturn V was ready. Apollo 7's mission was to put the mooncraft through a full flight test and give the service module's engine a rigorous reliability test. At 11:03 A.M. on October 11, Apollo 7 climbed

smoothly into orbit atop a Saturn IB. In the next 11 days, the crew fired the service module's rocket eight times, each time perfectly. They checked all of the ship's systems thoroughly, practiced rendezvous maneuvers and conducted telecasts for their earth-bound audience.

On October 22, after 163 orbits of a near-perfect mission, Apollo 7 splashed down in the Atlantic south of Bermuda. One delighted NASA official termed the mission a "101 per cent success."

Just as the Americans resumed their manned space operations, so did the Russians. Soyuz was successfully flown with a man aboard. Two modified Soyuz, called Zond, were sent unmanned around the moon and back. It looked as if the Soviet Union was about to snatch some of the glory from Apollo by sending a man around the moon.

But Apollo 8 clinched the moon race for the United States. Faced with a delay in the preparation of the lunar module, NASA changed its plans—and in doing so upstaged any last-minute Soviet challenge. Apollo 8, originally meant to test the LM around the earth, was to head for the moon on the first manned launch of a Saturn V. Colonel Frank Borman, the 40-year-old veteran of Gemini 7, was to command the crew. With him were James A. Lovell, Jr., his Gemini 7 crewmate, and a 35-year-old rookie astronaut, Major William A. Anders.

At 7:51 A.M. on December 21, 1968, the giant Saturn V on launch pad 39-A ignited its 7.5-million-pound-thrust engines and rose slowly into the sky. After 11½ minutes, Apollo 8 was in a 118-mile-high orbit around the earth. The astronauts checked all the instruments in their spacecraft. Satisfied with its condition, they re-ignited the third-stage booster over Hawaii and set course for the moon.

Within three months of the American tragedy disaster struck Russia's space program. Vladimir Komarov was killed on the re-entry stage of his flight in Soyuz 1, the first of a new series of spacecraft, when the parachutes failed to open.

Left: astronauts of Apollo 7 took this picture of the top stage of their Saturn IB booster, which had lifted them into orbit from Cape Canaveral, seen 150 miles below. They practiced rendezvous maneuvers with this booster in preparation for later flights that would actually carry a lunar module.

About 30 minutes after the "translunar injection," Apollo 8 jettisoned its third-stage booster and the dummy LM that had been carried along to simulate a full Apollo mooncraft. Apollo's trajectory was planned so that if the rocket in the service module failed, the spacecraft would still be swung around by the moon's gravity and return safely to earth.

At 3:30 P.M. on December 23, Apollo 8 crossed into the moon's gravitational field. The astronauts were now some 214,000 miles from earth. At this point, they turned the spacecraft to point the service module's big rocket toward the moon. For Apollo 8 to go into lunar orbit, the rocket would have to slow them down from 5,760 mph to 3,645 mph. At 4:49 A.M. on Christmas Eve, Apollo 8 passed behind the edge of the moon.

Precisely 10 minutes later, while the spacecraft was hidden on the far side of the moon, the big rocket fired perfectly. Twenty minutes later, Apollo 8 emerged from behind the moon. The controllers at Mission Control anxiously checked the data coming from the spacecraft. Orbit had been achieved.

For the next hour or so, the astronauts described their impressions of the moon's face to Mission Control at Houston. They called it "gray," "colorless," "barren," "a vast, lonely forbidding sight," "not a very inviting place." They pointed their small television camera down at the barren lunar surface and gave the people of earth their first closeup view of the moon.

After 10 orbits in about 20 hours, Apollo 8 was ready to return to earth. At 1:10 A.M., while behind the moon, the crew ignited their big rocket for the crucial burn that would blast them back out of lunar orbit and on their way home. The 20,500-pound thrust engine responded perfectly. As the spacecraft emerged from the back of the moon, Lovell announced the successful rocket firing to Houston this way: "Please be informed there is a Santa Claus."

The trip home took 57 hours. On the morning of December 27, 1968, Apollo 8 began its fiery re-entry into the earth's atmosphere at 24,530 miles per hour. At the edge of the atmosphere, the command module separated from the service module for the final descent. Small

A Saturn V rocket, the most powerful space launcher ever built, ascends on a pillar of flame. At its top is the Apollo's conical command module, the only part which returned to earth.

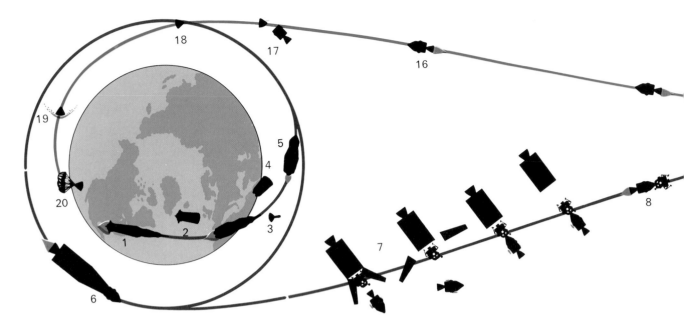

How Apollo got to the moon. The complex sequence of events which led to the greatest success of the space age.

1. Launch of Saturn V
2. 1st stage jettisoned, 2nd stage ignites
3. Launch escape tower jettisoned
4. 2nd stage jettisoned, 3rd stage ignites
5. Engine cutoff, 3rd stage enters earth parking orbit
6. 3rd stage re-ignites and begins translunar injection
7. Transposition and docking of the command service module (CSM) and lunar module (LM), 3rd stage jettisoned
8. Mid-course correction
9. CSM engine retro-fired for insertion into lunar orbit
10. Crew transfer and separation of CSM and LM
11. LM makes a powered descent and touch down
12. Launch of LM ascent stage
13. Rendezvous and docking of CSM and LM ascent stage
14. Crew transfer and jettison of LM ascent stage
15. CSM engine re-ignites and begins course toward earth
16. Mid-course correction
17. Separation of command module
18. CM enters crucial re-entry corridor
19. CM re-enters atmosphere
20. Parachutes deployed—splashdown

Right: the Apollo 8 astronauts splashed down to an enthusiastic reception. All three men were honored as the first men to leave the earth and circle the moon.

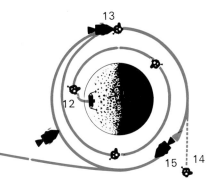

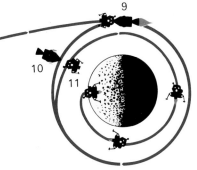

automatic thrusters on the command module fired occasionally to control and smooth the ride through the atmosphere. After 8 minutes, the spacecraft had slowed to 300 mph at 23,300 feet altitude. Three small parachutes emerged to pull out the three main chutes. Fourteen minutes after re-entry began, Apollo 8 splashed down in the Pacific, only four miles from the main recovery ship, the aircraft carrier *Yorktown*. Man had traveled round the moon and returned safely to earth.

One vital component of the Apollo moon-landing plans remained to be tested in manned flight—the lunar module (LM), which would actually take men to the surface and off again. This was the task of Apollo 9 with James McDivitt, the 39-year-old Gemini 4 veteran, in command. The second crew member, the navigator, was David R. Scott, who had made his first spaceflight in Gemini 8. He had written his master's thesis on interplanetary navigation at the Massachusetts Institute of Technology. Russell L. "Rusty" Schweickart, a 33-year-old civilian space rookie, was the third Apollo 9 crew member.

On March 3, 1969, Apollo 9 went smoothly into earth orbit. Scott turned the command and service modules to dock with the lunar module and extract it from the Saturn rocket's top stage. That stage was then re-fired to send it into an orbit around the sun. McDivitt and

During the flight of Apollo 9 the vital lunar module was first tested. With McDivitt and Schweickart on board, the LM freed itself from the command module and embarked on its first independent journey in space.

Schweickart moved into the lunar module and began to test its systems, particularly its descent engine. On day four, Schweickart made a space walk to try out the all-important lunar spacesuit and back pack that would keep astronauts alive while exploring the moon. His verdict: "The suit is very comfortable."

The critical and dangerous flight test for the LM began the next day on Apollo 9's 59th orbit. McDivitt and Schweickart were back in the LM. Then Scott on the command module cut them loose. The LM was on its own.

For the first hour, the two spacecraft stayed within a few miles of each other as they tested their rendezvous radars and guidance systems. Then McDivitt ignited the LM's descent rocket, taking it 100 miles from the command module. After several more hours of flying, it was time to attempt the all-important rendezvous. McDivitt jettisoned the LM's lower stage, the part that would be left on the lunar surface, and then fired the ascent engine just as the astronauts would have to do to leave

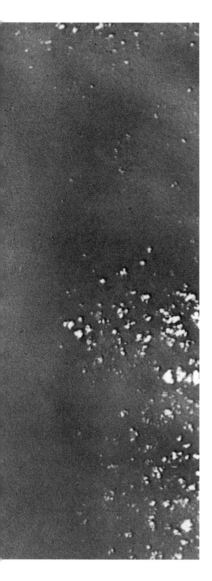

the moon. Both the rocket and the rendezvous radars worked perfectly. After 6½ hours of separation, the two spacecraft rendezvoused and docked. McDivitt and Schweickart returned to the safety of the command module and the LM was jettisoned. They flew the command module down to a precision splashdown in the Pacific only three miles from the waiting recovery ship.

Now there was a great deal of pressure within official NASA circles to achieve the manned lunar landing on the very next mission, Apollo 10, tentatively scheduled for May. But the Apollo Program Director, General Samuel Phillips, ruled otherwise. There had been only one flight to the moon so far and only one manned flight of the LM, and that had been in earth orbit. That was not sufficient flight experience, Phillips decided, to justify taking the enormous risks in attempting a manned lunar landing. One more dress rehearsal was needed.

In effect, Apollo 10 would perform all the maneuvers for a manned lunar landing except the final descent to the moon's surface. It was

Without the "umbilical cord" used by other astronauts, Russell Schweickart stepped outside the lunar module of Apollo 9. He inserted his feet into two specially designed restraints to keep him in contact with the spaceship.

nevertheless the most dangerous mission attempted thus far in the Apollo program. It combined all of the dangers of the Apollo 8 and 9 missions with additional uncertainties about the LM's behavior in lunar orbit and on its low passes over the lunar surface. Tom Stafford, a 38-year-old veteran of two Gemini flights, 6 and 9, was selected as command pilot. His crew were 35-year-old Eugene Cernan, Stafford's crewmate on Gemini 9, and John Young, another two-time veteran.

On May 18, right on schedule, Apollo 10 set off for the moon. Duplicating the Apollo 9 maneuvers, it linked with the LM, then

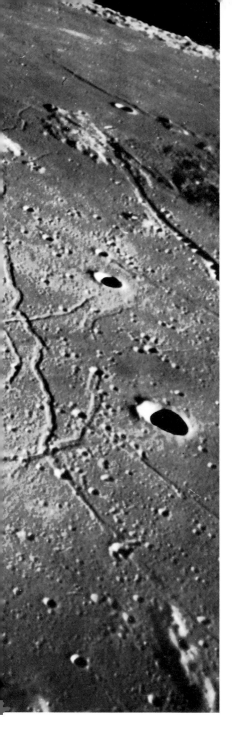

Apollo 10's 69-mile-high lunar
orbit offered man his closest look at
the moon's surface and the proposed
Apollo 11 lunar landing site. This picture
of the Triesnecker Crater is a northwest
view.

jettisoned its third-stage booster. At 4:45 P.M. on May 21, while traveling behind the moon, Apollo 10's service module rocket fired perfectly to place the spacecraft into a 69-mile-high lunar orbit.

On the morning of May 22, Stafford and Cernan crawled through the tunnel into the LM and separated it from the command module. They fired the descent rocket, and plunged down toward the lunar surface, to an orbit only 47,000 feet (about 9 miles) above the moon. The low pass was more than just a check of the LM, it was also a scouting expedition. The orbit was designed to carry the astronauts directly over the Sea of Tranquility, the primary landing site selected by the Apollo planners. Looking out of his window at man's closest view ever of the proposed landing site, Stafford described the surface as "very smooth, like wet clay."

As they approached Tranquility for their second pass, the astronauts fired the explosive bolts that would jettison the LM's lower descent stage. This would enable them to fire the ascent rocket for the return to the command module in exactly the same way as it would be done after a landing on the lunar surface. Suddenly something went wrong. Just as the lower stage was jettisoned, the upper stage with the astronauts inside began spinning wildly, pitching out of control. Stafford took over the manual controls and after about a minute was able to steady the spacecraft. Later, engineers were able to determine that the trouble had come from a switch which had been inadvertently left in the wrong position by workmen, but at that moment Project Apollo seemed terrifyingly close to another tragedy.

After making the second pass, the little LM smoothly rocketed up to a rendezvous with the command module. On May 24, having successfully completed the planned 31 orbits, Apollo 10 blasted out of lunar orbit and headed for home. At 12:52 P.M. on May 26, the spacecraft splashed down in the South Pacific within sight of the recovery aircraft carrier. There would be no more rehearsals. Within an hour after the astronauts stepped onto the carrier, Thomas O. Paine, NASA's administrator, made the historic announcement: "Eight years ago yesterday, the United States made the decision to land a man on the moon and return him safely by the end of the decade. Today, this moment, with the Apollo 10 crew safely aboard the U.S.S. *Princeton*, we know we can go to the moon; we will go to the moon. Tom Stafford, John Young, and Gene Cernan have given us the final confidence to make this bold step."

On the Moon
8

9:32 A.M. Eastern Daylight time, July 16, 1969. Pad 39-A, Kennedy Space Center, Florida. The giant Apollo moon rocket, 363 feet high and 6½ million pounds in weight, stood silhouetted against the clear Florida sky. In the command module high atop the great rocket, three men lay on their couches, waiting tensely for liftoff.

On the left-hand couch was 38-year-old Neil Alden Armstrong, the Apollo 11 commander. He had been a civilian test pilot before becoming an astronaut in 1962. On the center couch was 38-year-old Michael Collins, an Air Force Lieutenant Colonel. He would pilot the command module in moon orbit while the LM went down to the lunar surface and back again. On the right-hand couch was 39-year-old Edwin Eugene "Buzz" Aldrin, an Air Force Colonel. He would accompany Armstrong to the lunar surface.

On the beaches, in the various observation areas several miles distant, and on the roads leading to the Cape, nearly a million people strained their eyes to see the great rocket. Around the nation, around the world, hundreds of millions of people watched it on their television sets.

The giant rocket engines ignited. The force of the 7.5-million-pound rocket thrust shook the earth. Apollo 11 began to rise slowly, gradually picking up speed as it climbed into the sky. Right on schedule, Apollo 11 entered earth orbit, blasted into its translunar trajectory, docked with the LM and jettisoned the spent booster. On Friday, July 18, Armstrong and Aldrin crawled into the LM, which they had named *Eagle*, and took viewers at home on a color-television inspection tour of the little moonbug. *Eagle's* companion on the voyage was the command module *Columbia*.

The three-day trip to the moon was fairly uneventful. The astronauts followed the routine that had been established on the Apollo 8 and 10 missions. Some extra excitement was generated by the U.S.S.R. which on July 13, three days before Apollo 11's liftoff, had launched its own spacecraft Luna 15 to the moon. The Russians would tell the world nothing about the nature of the spacecraft's mission. But on July 18, the Russians informed the United States that their own un-manned spaceship, already in lunar orbit, would not interfere with Apollo 11.

Astronaut Irwin of Apollo 15 gives the salute to the American flag on the mission that first used a self-propelled lunar roving vehicle, seen here at the far right of the picture.

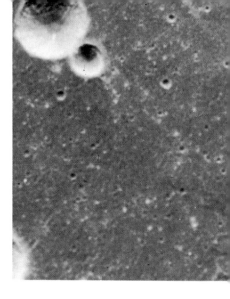

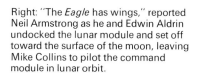

Right: "The *Eagle* has wings," reported Neil Armstrong as he and Edwin Aldrin undocked the lunar module and set off toward the surface of the moon, leaving Mike Collins to pilot the command module in lunar orbit.

Below right: view from the LM *Eagle* as it began its descent to the lunar surface. Armstrong took manual control of *Eagle* when he saw that the landing site was littered with boulders.

The giant Saturn V rocket blasted off carrying Apollo 11 and its crew of Neil Armstrong, Mike Collins, and Edwin Aldrin, to make man's first moon landing.

On Saturday, July 19, Apollo 11 swung into orbit around the moon. On the morning of Sunday, July 20, Armstrong and Aldrin crawled through the 30-inch-wide tunnel into *Eagle*. At 1:45 P.M. the two spacecraft undocked. "The *Eagle* has wings," Armstrong reported to Houston.

The two spacecraft separated and then passed behind the moon where *Eagle's* descent engine would fire to start the LM on an arching trajectory to a landing on the Sea of Tranquility. At 3:46 P.M. the spacecraft emerged from behind the moon. "The burn was on time," reported Armstrong matter-of-factly. The spacecraft was at an altitude of about 20 miles, descending toward 50,000 feet. At that point, the astronauts had to make the all-important final decision whether to remain in orbit or to initiate powered descent to the lunar surface to make the landing.

At about 4:07 P.M., the computer signaled that the 50,000-foot altitude had been reached—the pilot had five seconds to make his decision. Neil Armstrong pressed a button marked "Proceed." The descent engine ignited and the spacecraft started downward. After seven minutes, the spacecraft was 21,000 feet above the lunar surface and only five miles from the touchdown target. With less than two minutes until touchdown, the spacecraft was only 500 feet above the lunar surface. Looking down on the landing site. Armstrong suddenly saw, to his horror, that the computer-controlled guidance system was taking him and his companion right down into what he later described as a "football-field-sized crater with a large number of big boulders and rocks." Armstrong quickly took manual control of the spacecraft. Precious seconds passed as the astronaut searched for a clear area amid the menacing rock field below him. At last he sighted one and gently eased the LM down. At 4:17 P.M. the LM touched down on the surface of the moon.

"Houston," Armstrong radioed, "Tranquility base here. The *Eagle* has landed."

Apollo 11 was safely on the lunar surface. For the first time, men from earth had touched down on another celestial body. But the mission—and the commitment—were far from over. Armstrong and

Stepping onto the moon Armstrong told the world, "The surface is fine and powdery . . . I can see footprints of my boots . . . in the fine sandy particles."

Aldrin still had to get off the lunar surface, back to the command module, and back to earth. In the meantime, there was scientific work to be done.

Before stepping out onto the moon, the two astronauts had to make a careful check of their spacecraft to be sure that *Eagle* had suffered no damage during the landing. This kept them occupied for much of the next 6 hours. Finally, at 10:56 P.M. on Sunday, July 20, 1969, Neil Armstrong opened *Eagle's* hatch, descended the ladder, and became the first human to set foot on the lunar surface. As his left foot touched the moon to take the first step, he spoke the now famous sentence, "That's one small step for a man, one giant leap for mankind."

Aldrin stepped out onto the moon 18 minutes later, after handing down much of the equipment they would both need for their work. Every move the two men made on the moon was watched on television by millions of people throughout the world, half of whom were staying up all night to watch.

Armstrong said that the lunar surface was fine and powdery, like powdered charcoal, and described how it adhered in a thin layer to the soles and sides of his boots. He later compared it to powdered graphite on earth. *Eagle's* foot pads sank only 1 or 2 inches into the lunar surface, he said. His own footprints were not much more than an eighth of an inch deep.

They had landed on a fairly level plain in the Sea of Tranquility, about 4 miles farther west along their flight path than had been planned. Armstrong described the plain as a field of circular secondary craters, most of them ranging from 5 to 50 feet in diameter. In addition, there were, he said, "literally thousands" of 1- and 2-foot craters all around him.

The two astronauts observed a wide variety of "angular" blocks and boulders, generally about 2 feet high. They all seemed to be coated with the grayish white fine dust that gives the lunar surface its "dirty beach" appearance. The broken rocks, however, showed much darker interiors. Others were full of tiny holes.

Of all the astronauts' duties during their two hours on the lunar surface, collecting rock and soil samples was considered the most important. Armstrong's first job after he stepped onto the moon was to scoop up a "contingency sample" of lunar soil and place it in the leg pocket of his spacesuit. This was to ensure that scientists on the ground would have at least some lunar material to work with even if the astronauts had to cancel their prolonged "moonwalk." As it happened,

the astronauts collected 50 pounds of samples.

The astronauts placed three scientific experiments on the lunar surface. One was a seismometer—an instrument to measure earth-quake-like shocks on the moon. During the LM's liftoff, this instrument reported the expected tremors from the spacecraft engine, and then reported continuing tremors for many minutes afterward.

Another experiment left on the lunar surface was a reflector composed of 100 fused silica prisms arranged in a 2-foot square which the astronauts left pointing toward the earth. After the Apollo 11 flight was over, scientists bounced a laser beam from the earth off this reflector and then back to earth again, to obtain a precise measurement of the

Checking the LM to see if any damage had occurred during the landing, Armstrong reported that everything was fine: "The descent engine did not leave a crater on the ground . . . I'm looking up at Buzz in the windows . . . and I can see everything quite clearly."

distance between the moon and the earth.

A third experiment involved the solar wind, the continuous stream of particles and gases coming out of the sun. The solar wind had first been detected by unmanned satellites around the earth. The two astronauts set up a sheet of metal foil to trap some of the rare gases coming from the sun. The gas sample was then placed in a special box and carried back to earth for analysis by scientists.

While performing these tasks, Armstrong reported that it seemed easier than expected to work on the surface in his 185-pound spacesuit and that he was quite comfortable, despite temperatures ranging from between 240 and 250°F in the sunlight to minus 150°F in the shadows. Aldrin tested a number of means of moving about the lunar surface including a "kangaroo hop," but came to the conclusion that conventional walking or loping seemed the best. Both astronauts reported having trouble in adjusting their eyes to the glare, particularly as they stepped from shadows into sunlight.

Before they climbed back into *Eagle,* Armstrong and Aldrin planted an American flag, but because there is no atmosphere on the moon to hold up the flag, the banner was held unfurled by wires. There was also a plaque with the words "HERE MEN FROM THE PLANET EARTH FIRST SET FOOT UPON THE MOON JULY 1969 A.D. WE CAME IN PEACE FOR ALL MANKIND," and their signatures, together with President Nixon's, engraved on it. The plaque was attached to one of the legs of the LM's lower descent stage, which would remain on the moon when they left. The last relic of their voyage was a replica of their Apollo 11 insignia with an olive branch. By 1:09 A.M. July 21, 1969 astronauts Armstrong and Aldrin had concluded man's first moon walk and retired to the *Eagle* for a well-earned rest.

A little over 12 hours later, at 1:54 P.M. *Eagle's* engine ignited and the LM's ascent stage began to rise. "Beautiful...very smooth, very quiet ride," Armstrong reported. Minutes later, *Eagle* was in orbit. At about 3:30 P.M. *Columbia* appeared around the near side of the moon in its 26th orbit. *Eagle* was 7.7 miles behind and closing. For the next 2 hours, the two spacecraft maneuvered closer and closer to each other. At 5:35 P.M., some 69 miles above the lunar surface, *Eagle* and *Columbia* docked.

Armstrong and Aldrin could not re-enter the command module immediately. Everything they had brought up from the lunar surface was covered with the fine moondust. For more than an hour, the astronauts carefully vacuumed the dust from their sample cases,

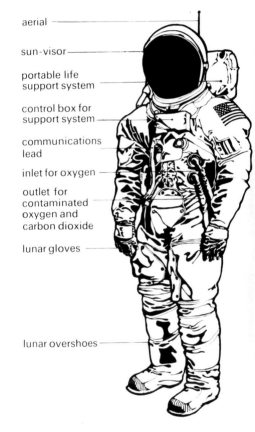

aerial

sun-visor

portable life
support system

control box for
support system

communications
lead

inlet for oxygen

outlet for
contaminated
oxygen and
carbon dioxide

lunar gloves

lunar overshoes

The moonwalk suit was worked out to provide the greatest comfort and convenience possible for the astronauts outside the lunar module. Almost as self-sufficient as a spacecraft, the suit carried its own atmosphere and protected against vacuum, extremes of temperature, or puncture by stray micrometeoroids. The astronaut was able to walk, dig, or climb, but could only reach an inch or so above his head or down as far as his knees.

The Apollo 11 LM *Eagle* rises from the surface of the moon to rendezvous with its command module *Columbia*. The docking was successful, and the world's first lunarnauts started home.

equipment, and clothing. Finally, at 7:20 P.M. *Columbia* reported: "We're all three back inside." *Columbia* then jettisoned *Eagle* and at 12 : 55 A.M., July 22, fired its service module engine to blast out of lunar orbit.

The flight back was quiet. At 12 : 50 P.M. Apollo 11 splashed down in the South Pacific 950 miles southwest of Hawaii and 11 miles from their recovery ship, the U.S.S. *Hornet*. Man had landed on the moon and safely returned.

As the recovery ship U.S.S. *Hornet* closed in on the Apollo 11 command module bobbing in the Pacific swell, over 4000 miles away at the Kennedy Space Center, preparations were already in hand for NASA's second manned lunar landing. Another giant Saturn stood at the doors of the Vehicle Assembly Building ready for its $3\frac{1}{2}$-mile journey to pad 39-A. Astronauts Charles "Pete" Conrad, Alan Bean,

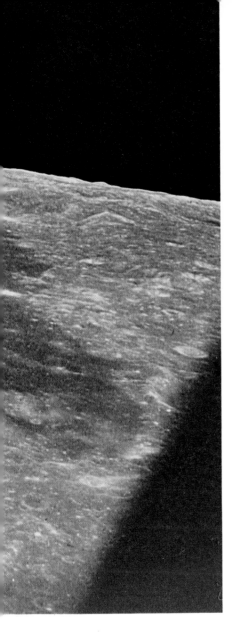

The distance of intimacy

What do you talk about, crammed into that tiny cockpit with two other men in the vastness of space? As Apollo 11 sped toward the moon, conversation was limited almost exclusively to technical jargon. Collins, Buzz Aldrin and Neil Armstrong were remarkably free from quarrels, but they were not close friends. Neil Armstrong's wife described her husband as "silent. The word 'no' is an argument." Perhaps, as Aldrin admits, they have been "dehumanized" by the treadmill of the space program.

Six years after the moon flight, Armstrong told an interviewer that he was too busy doing his job when he landed on the moon to ponder the cosmic meanings of what it was all about. Aldrin still insists that he—and not Armstrong—should have been first to walk on the moon. When he heard that Armstrong was to be the first, he asked his fellow astronaut if this were true. "Neil equivocated a minute or so, and then with a coolness I had not known he possessed, he said that the decision was quite historic and he didn't want to rule out the possibility of going first." Aldrin never recovered from being second. After his return from the moon he became deeply depressed and divorced his wife of 17 years.

When Apollo 11 splashed down in the South Pacific, Armstrong, Aldrin, and Collins were hurried directly into quarantine in case they had brought back any moon germs to the earth.

Diagram shows the sequence of events
that saved the three astronauts in
Apollo 13 from the brink of disaster:

1. Explosion in oxygen tank
2. Lovell and Haise move into LM,
   using LM motor to power spacecraft;
   Swigert joins them later
3. Radio contact lost
4. LM engine restarted
5. Service module jettisoned. Astronauts
   transfer to command module
   LM jettisoned
6. Re-entry into earth's atmosphere
7. Splashdown, 4 miles off course

and Richard Gordon were approaching the final phases of training and looking forward to their launch date, November 14. Before the jubilation surrounding Apollo 11's success had even begun to subside, NASA was almost ready for its next big test, Apollo 12.

When the mission was flown, it came almost as an anticlimax. Not only was it a perfect flight, but the irrepressible good humor of the crew was a sharp contrast to the tight-lipped approach of the Apollo 11 astronauts. In particular, lunar module pilot Alan Bean and mission commander Pete Conrad conducted their lunar Extra Vehicular Activities (EVA's) with unmistakable delight. Their touchdown in the Ocean of Storms had been perfect. Conrad and Bean even found time to make a joke or two in the final moments of descent. It was the first time NASA had attempted a pinpoint landing, but the two astronauts handled the LM *Intrepid* with absolute precision.

Bean and Gordon spent a total of 7 hours and 39 minutes on the lunar surface in the course of two EVA's, and gathered 75 pounds of lunar samples. In addition they deployed the first Apollo Lunar Surface Experiments Package (ALSEP). They also made an 80-yard journey to examine an early unmanned U.S. moon probe, Surveyor 3. They photographed the probe and removed parts of its TV camera and scoop equipment for analysis by scientists on earth. The mission's only serious disappointment came while Bean was setting up the color TV camera. He inadvertently turned the lens toward the sun, the delicate element was burned out almost instantly, and earthbound viewers were deprived of a glimpse of Bean and Gordon at work.

Apollo 12 went almost too smoothly, but it was not long before the world was reminded of the hazards of spaceflight. The relaxed good humor of Apollo 12's crew had lulled people into thinking that the rest of the moon flights were to be mere routine. Apollo 13 soon destroyed the illusion. Rookie astronauts Fred Haise and John Swigert, and space veteran Jim Lovell were lucky to return with their lives.

Early Monday evening, April 13, 1970, just two days after liftoff, Lovell and Haise passed from the command module (*Odyssey*) through the connecting tunnel to check the LM's systems prior to the forthcoming landing. Suddenly, as Lovell was moving back through the tunnel from *Aquarius*, an explosion shook the ship. The astronauts scrambled to the command module's instruments. One of the main electrical systems was losing power rapidly. Through the ports the men could see that gas was being vented into space from somewhere back in the service module. Swigert quickly radioed Houston with the

words that were to transform an uneventful flight into a grim struggle for survival: "Hey, we've got a problem here!"

Following a rapid exchange between flight controllers at Houston and the three men over 200,000 miles out in space, the situation became clear. Pressure in one of the Apollo 13's two oxygen tanks had dropped to zero. Together with the hydrogen tanks, the oxygen tanks fed three fuel cells housed in the service module. The cells provided the power for all vital ship functions, including life support and guidance. Within a few minutes the command module would be unable to keep the astronauts alive. Coupled with this, the main propulsion engine in the service module was inoperable. The position was critical.

Almost immediately, Houston announced that Lovell, Haise and Swigert were going to use the LM *Aquarius* as a lifeboat. They would shut down *Odyssey* and power up the LM's systems, which were, however, designed only for that lunar landing phase of the flight. Anxiety for the three astronauts was felt throughout the world.

Still three days away from the earth, the astronauts transferred to *Aquarius*. The only power remaining to the command module was emergency battery power. This would be needed in the last stages of the nightmare flight. Only the command module could return through

Above: the perilous spaceflight is nearly over as parachutes carry the Apollo 13 command module toward the South Pacific recovery area.

Above left: Apollo 13's service module suffered a crippling explosion that could have meant death for its crew. Seeing the damage, one astronaut exclaimed in surprise: "There's one whole side of the spacecraft missing . . . man, that's unbelievable."

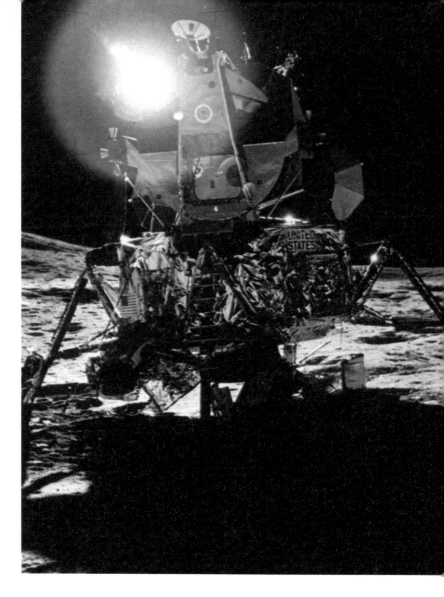

Above: Alan Shepard, who had been America's first man in space, at age 49 became America's oldest man in space as commander of the Apollo 14 mission.

Below: a lunar sample brought back by Apollo 14. In 33½ hours on the surface of the moon, astronauts returned a record 96 pounds of samples.

the earth's atmosphere, and the lifeboat *Aquarius* would have to be discarded before re-entry.

When the astronauts made the transfer, they were 20 hours out from the moon. Houston instructed them to use the LM's small descent engine to put themselves into a free-return trajectory. With no further effort apart from course-correction burns, the spacecraft would swing around the moon and on course for earth. But conditions aboard were becoming grueling. The need to conserve the LM's limited power supplies meant that cabin heating was kept to a minimum. Rest periods had been disrupted, so fatigue was added to the nervous strain the men were already under. Before long, a buildup of carbon dioxide in the cabin's atmosphere approached danger level. Under urgent instructions from Houston, the three men pirated parts from their spacesuits to make a lithium hydroxide air cleaner.

Early on April 15, Apollo 13 entered the influence of the earth's gravitational field, and began to accelerate. Some hours later, shortly before re-entry, the crippled service module was jettisoned—leaving

Apollo 14 on the moon's surface. The LM *Antares* landed in Fra Mauro, less than 60 yards from the designated spot. Alan Shepard and Edgar Mitchell completed two EVA's.

the command and lunar modules in a configuration never previously flown. The astronauts maneuvered their craft to examine the damage to the service module. A whole panel was blown out, almost from the base to the engine.

Shortly after, the command module was separated from the LM. Drawing on its last reserves of power, it plunged into the earth's atmosphere. Just 142 hours and 54 minutes after launch, Apollo 13 returned on target in the Pacific.

Although the mission had come close to tragedy, there was nonetheless an element of triumph. The vast manned spaceflight network had saved the lives of the crew. This, together with the resolute courage of the astronauts under tremendous stress, was a triumph of human effort and resourcefulness. But steps had to be taken to ensure that the explosion that wrecked Apollo 13 could never threaten another mission. A commission of inquiry was set up, headed by Neil Armstrong, and within three months, an exhaustive report was ready. As a result of the report, the service modules were modified, and extra safety facilities were built into the command modules.

Although the commission had worked with great speed and efficiency, the Apollo 14 mission originally planned for the summer of 1970 was delayed until January 31, 1971. NASA named the prime crew as Edgar Mitchell, Stuart Roosa—both space rookies—and 48-year-old Alan Shepard. Ten years earlier Shepard had become America's first man in space in the first Mercury space capsule. Now he was ready to become America's oldest man in space.

But a far greater significance surrounded Apollo 14. Almost as soon as NASA had achieved the primary task of the 1960's—to land the first men on the moon—public interest in moonflight had begun to wane. More important NASA's budgets were cut dramatically. Even before Apollo 14, NASA had reduced the program from the ten flights originally planned to seven. With the failure of Apollo 13, and with continued financial support in question, Apollo 14 could afford nothing less than total success.

Apollo 14's liftoff on January 31, 1971, was the start of a tense mission for NASA. In fact, within hours of the launch, it seemed that NASA's worst fears might be realized. Five thousand miles out in space, the command module had failed to dock with the LM *Antares*. Command module pilot Stuart Roosa patiently repeated the maneuver, but each time the docking failed. Then, on the sixth attempt, Roosa almost shouted over the radio link, "hard dock!" *Antares* and the command module *Kitty Hawk* were locked together. Some hours later, the moon landing still looked unlikely. NASA could not understand the source of the docking problem. If it happened again in moon orbit, the consequences might be disastrous. Eventually, however, after long deliberation, Houston announced that the landing was on. By February 3, Shepard and Mitchell were aboard *Antares*, starting the descent stage engine. Minutes later, they had landed in Fra Mauro less than 60 yards from the planned spot.

Shepard and Mitchell made two EVA's. The first, lasting 4 hours and 50 minutes, involved deploying the ALSEP, gathering soil samples, and detonating a series of 21 small explosive charges that were registered as slight moon tremors on three especially arranged geophones. Despite using a cart to carry equipment, the astronauts rapidly tired. Eventually they had to return to *Antares* without completing all their tasks. During the second EVA, lasting 4 hours and 35 minutes, the problem of fatigue became critical. As the two men laboriously climbed the sloping sides of nearby Cone Crater, Shepard began to falter. The two men turned back.

After $33\frac{1}{2}$ hours on the moon, *Antares* lifted off to join *Kitty Hawk*. Docking went perfectly, and on February 9, Apollo 14 splashed down safely. It returned a record 96 pounds of lunar samples.

Apollo 15, launched on July 26, represented a major step in the Apollo program. It was the first of the "J" missions, characterized by extremely high scientific content and the use of a self-propelled lunar

The rigors of space flight

The training was intense. The worst part was a "diabolical" device known as a centrifuge, designed to imitate the acceleration experienced riding a rocket into space by swinging a small gondola, or imitation cockpit, round in a circle on a 50-foot arm. This "wheel" pushed the would-be astronauts to artificially high gravities up to 15 times greater than on earth. As the machines started to speed up, astronauts reported intense pain in the chest, followed by difficulty in breathing, as if steel bands were tightly encircling the chest. There was also training in subjects such as geology, and survival courses in case the spacecraft landed unexpectedly in a remote part of the world.

It was during this training period that the astronauts first donned spacesuits; not a pleasant experience. The spacesuit must be airtight to protect the astronaut from the vacuum of space. It must be pressurized to stop the fluid inside dissolving in a pool of sweat. It must have built-in communications devices. The gloves must be thin to allow manipulation of delicate controls. The helmet must be light and give excellent vision. In addition the suit must protect the astronaut against heat, cold and micrometeoroids.

Once in their spacesuits, the astronauts learned the lesson of weightlessness in a jetliner specially maneuvered to simulate zero gravity. They tried to drink out of paper cups—but at zero gravity the water floats out of the cups in great spherical blobs.

The training was tough because it needed to be. The inside of a Gemini is smaller than the front seat of a Volkswagen Beetle. You cannot get out of the seat because there is no place to go. To get the astronauts used to the spacecraft, a special flight simulator was built. Day after day was spent watching light on a darkened screen.

The food has improved since the early spaceflights when astronauts squeezed all their food from aluminum tubes. The men of Apollo 11 dined mainly on freeze-dried food, with normal

Apollo 15, launched in July 1971, used the lunar rover. It enabled Irwin, seen at the vehicle, and Scott to collect the richest scientific haul of the whole program.

slices of bread and sandwich spreads. For the moon landing, the astronauts' diets were worked out in consultation with their wives "to see what their husband's likes and preferences were." Sixty different dishes were finally made available. Cooking the meal was simple. The astronaut removed his aluminum-wrapped dinner from the storage bin and cut the cord to which all meals were attached. A small amount of hot water was inserted through a special nozzle and the package kneaded to reconstitute the food, which was eaten with a spoon.

There was no bathroom aboard the Apollo flights. Personal hygiene had to be kept with a minimum of privacy. Before the first space flight, scientists did not know whether an astronaut's elimination functions would work normally in zero G. When early space fliers proved that they did, the scientists set to work on devising ways to dispose and store body waste. To urinate, the men of Apollo 11 used a 100-inch flexible tube which terminated at an overboard dump valve in the wall of the module. Fluid freezes instantly in space—and this proved a problem at first as the outlet valve constantly jammed with ice. This was solved by fitting electric heater coils. Once in space, the frozen urine floated along with the spacecraft as tiny particles of ice.

Solid body waste was another problem. While wearing his "hard" spacesuit, the astronaut was equipped with a cloth and rubber nappy—which, it was hoped, he never had to use. The problem was far simpler while the spacecraft was pressurized and the astronaut wearing his casual glass-fibre suit. The suit was taken off and the adhesive top of a plastic bag, equipped with toilet paper and a wet-wipe cleansing tissue, fixed to the buttocks. Afterwards, a germicide was placed in the bag, which was sealed and stored in a special compartment for analysis back on earth. The only exception was in the lunar module, which had no overboard dump valve—and stored both urine and solid wastes in bags. Because of the weight problem during take-off from the moon, these bags were left behind on the surface.

The Apollo 16 Saturn V space vehicle carrying astronauts John Young, Thomas Mattingly and Charles Duke streaks spacewards from Florida at the start of NASA's eighth manned voyage to the moon. Liftoff was at 12.54 P.M. on April 16, 1972.

roving vehicle. The rover would enable the "J" mission astronauts to explore up to several miles away from their LM, and would remove the dangers of fatigue that had jeopardized Apollo 14. In fact, Apollo 15 carried over 40 million dollars worth of scientific equipment. The weight of equipment landed on the moon was increased from 250 pounds on Apollo 14, to over 1000 pounds. The mission was flown by astronauts David Scott, James Irwin, and Alfred Worden. Scott and Irwin took the LM *Falcon* to a perfect landing close to the spectacular, canyonlike Hadley Rille. Worden remained aboard the command module *Endeavour*, conducting a long series of observations and experiments.

During their 66 hour and 55 minute stay on the moon, Scott and Irwin explored the lunar surface for a total of 18 hours and 36 minutes, and retrieved 170 pounds of lunar samples. The battery-powered lunar rover performed superbly. It transformed the EVA's, giving the two men a mobility that allowed a thorough exploration of the terrain surrounding their landing site. After the third EVA, the astronauts left the moon with the richest scientific haul of the Apollo program.

The penultimate Apollo mission, Apollo 16, was the first to land in the lunar highlands, where scientists expected to find samples of the

ancient lunar crust dating back to the origin of the moon. Launched on April 16, 1972, Apollo 16 was crewed by John Young, Charles Duke, and Thomas Mattingly. In the lunar module *Orion*, Young and Duke touched down near the crater Descartes. But instead of finding original lunar crust as expected, they found themselves walking on rocks which had been fragmented and ejected from one of the large impacts which shaped the moon's features. This gave scientists a fascinating new insight into the violent history of the lunar surface. The Apollo 16 astronauts spent a total of 20 hours 14 minutes exploring the moon, collecting 213 pounds of samples.

After Apollo 16, only one mission remained—Apollo 17's flight to the Taurus-Littrow region, where bright lunar hills meet dark lunar lowlands. Here might lie many clues to the moon's history. Following launch on December 7, 1972, crewmen Eugene Cernan, civilian scientist Harrison "Jack" Schmitt, and Ronald Evans flew a perfect mission. Cernan and Schmitt made the exciting discovery of orange-colored soil, produced by iron-rich glassy beads fused in the heat of a meteoroid impact. Fittingly, to end the series, Apollo 17 set up a host of records including time spent on the moon (75 hours in total, of which Cernan and Schmitt spent 22 hours exploring the

The flame from the Apollo 16 lunar module *Orion* ascent engine created a kaleidoscope effect during the liftoff from the moon, as seen in this reproduction from a color television transmission from a camera mounted on the lunar roving vehicle.

Right: one of the most exciting
Apollo 17 discoveries was orange-
colored soil, produced as a result of a
meteoroid impact.

Below: the Taurus-Littrow region of
the moon, surveyed by the Apollo 17
mission, is where bright lunar hills
meet dark lunar lowlands. From the
samples taken, it was hoped to find
many clues to the moon's history.

surface), distance driven in the lunar rover (22 miles), and weight of samples collected (250 pounds).

On December 11, 1972, Apollo 17 splashed down safely in the Pacific Ocean. The last men had returned from the moon. Project Apollo had finished. It all seemed something of an anticlimax.

What did the total 805 pounds of lunar samples, and other information returned by the Apollo astronauts, tell scientists about the moon? Firstly, the most astounding thing about the moon rocks was their extreme age. The very youngest, those collected on the Apollo 12 mission, were 3,200 million years old, far older than most rocks on earth. The moon turned out to be warmer inside than expected, but not hot enough for any present-day volcanic activity.

As scientists worked their way through the moon rocks—and many of the samples will not be touched for years to come, so great is the task—the following picture emerged. The moon, like the rest of the solar system, formed 4,600 million years ago, probably as an independent body near the earth. Early in its history it became molten and a crust formed, like scum. Then, as the moon cooled, it was bombarded by smaller bodies left over from the formation of the solar system. This bombardment fragmented the crust and dug out most of the major features we see today. About 3,900 million years ago, the bombardment ceased. For the next 500 million years or so, lavas oozed out from within the moon to form the dark lowland plains. And then the moon died. Apart from an occasional impact that dug a new crater, the moon has scarcely changed for the past 3,000 million years.

The Apollo 17 astronauts brought back 250 pounds of lunar samples. In all, they spent 75 hours on the moon's surface, 22 of them exploring outside the lunar module.

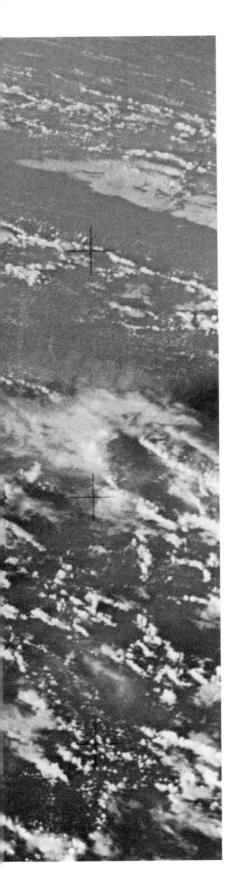

Stations in Space

9

It was the biggest load ever launched into space—and perhaps it was too much to expect that everything would go according to plan. The idea was to orbit a space station where three American astronauts could experience what a long spaceflight would be like—while carrying out various observations and experiments.

The solution was Skylab, made from the converted top stage of a Saturn V rocket. Its main section was a cylinder 48 feet long and 22 feet in diameter, divided into two sections: a laboratory where the astronauts worked, and crew quarters where they ate, slept and relaxed. The workshop was connected by an airlock to a small cylinder known as the docking adaptor, which contained two docking ports for Apollo spacecraft—one for a rescue should an emergency arise—and also housed control consoles for a battery of solar telescopes mounted at its side.

Weighing 75 tons and measuring over 80 feet, Skylab became the world's biggest and heaviest space payload when it was launched without a crew into a 170-mile-high orbit on May 14, 1973. But ironically, Skylab's launch was almost its downfall. As the rocket thundered into the sky, the force of air rushing past it tore off a shield intended to protect Skylab from meteoroids in space. Along with the shield went one of the wing-like solar panels that were meant to open in orbit to provide the space station with electrical power; another wing was jammed by debris. Without these panels Skylab was depleted of power when in orbit. It also began to overheat, because the meteoroid shield had been intended to act as a sunshield.

NASA officials canceled the launch of the first Skylab crew which had been planned for the following day, while they studied ways to save the stricken space station. On May 25, 1973, Charles Conrad and his crew of Joseph Kerwin and Paul Weitz took off from Cape Canaveral in an Apollo capsule to perform a repair mission that was to prove difficult, dangerous, and demanding. The first problem was in docking with the space station. Eight times Conrad approached the stricken Skylab—and eight times the docking latches failed to lock. Finally the tired men donned spacesuits to make an impromptu repair of the docking mechanism. On the ninth try they made it.

Skylab space station photographed in orbit 170 miles above the earth by the first crew of astronauts aboard the command/service module.

Above: Skylab space station, propelled by a modified Saturn V rocket, was launched on May 14, 1973.

The space mechanics had come equipped with a huge, delicate parasol with collapsible ribs intended to serve as a makeshift sunshade for Skylab. Cautiously they entered the space station—to find the temperature inside a merciless 130°F. They pushed the parasol out through one of the station's small airlocks and opened it. With the sunshade installed, temperatures inside Skylab began to fall to more comfortable levels.

Skylab was getting some electrical power from a windmill-like array of solar panels attached to the solar telescope mount, but more power was needed to operate all the experiments aboard the station. Conrad and Kerwin performed a daring spacewalk to cut free the jammed solar panel. As it swung into position, electrical power surged into the space station, ensuring the continued success of the mission. The Skylab astronauts had shown the value of man in space for performing running repairs.

Skylab was intended to answer a lot of unanswered questions about life in space, the most intriguing of which was the effect of continued weightlessness on the human body. How do you move around when your feet have no traction? Skylab's workshop was 27 feet long and 22 feet wide, with living quarters at one end equipped with an 18-inch window and built-in heaters for tinned and frozen foods. Three sleeping bags were fitted against the walls and the toilet was suction operated.

The first reports from Conrad reassured ground control: "Mobility around here is super. Nobody has motion sickness." After some initial

practice, the men soon became used to moving objects that would weigh more than 100 pounds on earth.

Is there an "up" and a "down" in a space Skylab? "Yes," reported Kerwin. "You do have a sense of up and down, and you can change it whenever it's convenient. If you go from one module into the other and you're upside down, you say to your brain 'I want that way to be up,' and your brain says 'okay.' It's strictly eyeballs and brain."

There were other problems. When the men opened containers of liquid food, droplets drifted into the room, clinging to instruments. Opening a drawer could be hazardous—objects inside tended to float out. And they had to shout to make themselves heard because sound carried poorly in Skylab's artificial atmosphere.

Above: Skylab space station in earth orbit, photographed by the first crew from their command/service module. The gold-colored sunshade shades the Orbital Workshop from which a meteoroid/sun shield has been missing since the launch in 1973. Also lost during the launch was the solar panel which should be on the right-hand side of the photograph.

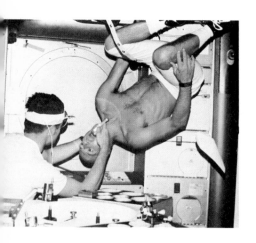

Astronaut Joseph Kerwin, a doctor, examines Charles Conrad, commander of the first Skylab crew, in the crew quarters of the Orbital Workshop. Conrad is able to float upside-down in the weightlessness of space.

The Skylab astronauts had a wide variety of tasks to perform. They used the Skylab telescopes to observe the sun, they monitored the surface of the earth, and they performed experiments that made use of the conditions of weightlessness in space. The solar telescopes were designed to observe the sun at ultra-violet and x-ray wavelengths, which do not penetrate the earth's atmosphere. At these wavelengths they could get a spectacular new view of the violent eruptions that rack the sun's surface, flinging plumes of intensely hot gas into space. Our own planet came under surveillance with cameras and radar, not for military purposes but to map its geology, ocean currents, weather patterns, and land usage. These observations extended and improved the work of existing unmanned satellites.

One of the most important uses of orbital stations in the future may be for the production of new materials unobtainable on earth, based on experiments that started in Skylab. Skylab was equipped with a furnace for melting and fusing metals and glass. In weightlessness, liquids can be made to mix that do not mix under the normal conditions of gravity on earth; and molten materials solidify with almost perfect homogeneity in weightlessness, because there is none of the effect of convection that occurs under gravity. As a result, new alloys and new types of glassy crystals used in electronics can be produced in space laboratories. These substances may possess desirable properties not otherwise obtainable. Another beneficial effect of the absence of gravity is that super-pure vaccines can be produced. Whole new electronic, metallurgical, and pharmaceutical industries may be established in orbit to take advantage of weightless conditions.

The first Skylab crew returned to earth after 28 days in space. On July 28, 1973, their places were taken by a second crew of Alan Bean, Owen Garriott, and Jack Lousma. One of Garriott and Lousma's tasks was a long spacewalk, during which they loaded new film into the solar observatory telescopes and spread out a new and larger sunshade over the original parasol installed by the first crew. This shade remained in place for the rest of the mission.

Among the experiments performed by the second crew were 17 that had been suggested by American high-school children in a special competition. One which attracted wide attention involved two spiders called Arabella and Anita, which were filmed as they tried to spin webs in unaccustomed weightlessness. After some initial disorientation, both spiders adapted quickly and spun webs similar to those they constructed on earth. In another student experiment, the swimming

Above: astronaut Owen Garriott
stationed at the controls of the solar
telescope in Skylab's multiple docking
adaptor.

Right: astronaut Garriott space-walking
beside Skylab's telescope mount.

ability of minnows was studied. Those brought from earth swam at first in tight loops, but those hatched from eggs in space swam normally right from the start.

The second Skylab crew returned to earth after two months in orbit. The third and last crew—Gerald Carr, Edward Gibson, and William Pogue—took off on November 16, 1973, for a record-breaking 12 weeks in space. A scientific bonus during their flight was the appearance of comet Kohoutek, a visitor from the depths of the solar system, which they were able to observe in detail.

They returned to earth on February 8, 1974, having brought the total Skylab scientific haul to 182,000 photographs of the sun and 40,000 photographs of the earth. All crews found that not only did they adapt readily to prolonged weightlessness, it was actually an enjoyable experience. Each crew regularly used an exercise bicycle and other devices to help keep fit in orbit, so they suffered no ill effects on their return to earth. Together, the three flight crews had spent 171 days 13 hours in orbit, traveled 70,500,000 miles, and spent 41 hours 46 minutes outside their spacecraft.

Skylab was abandoned in orbit after the third crew left. It was intended to remain aloft until the 1980's, when the Space Shuttle could rendezvous with it and push it into a higher orbit for re-use. But greater-than-expected atmospheric drag brought Skylab plunging to earth on July 11, 1979, scattering red-hot debris over the Australian outback.

Russian space exploits were all but eclipsed during the Apollo and Skylab successes. The Russians, too, were working toward the goal of long-duration space stations, but they were dogged by failure. Their first space station, Salyut 1, was launched on April 19, 1971. Salyut was modified from the top stage of the largest Russian launch rocket, called Proton. It was in the shape of three interconnected cylinders with a maximum diameter of 13½ feet and a total length of 39 feet. Salyut's internal volume was one quarter that of Skylab.

Russian cosmonauts were ferried to and from Salyut in Soyuz spacecraft. Soyuz had been introduced in 1967, but its maiden flight ended in the death of its pilot, Vladimir Komarov, when it went out of control during re-entry. Subsequent missions were devoted to testing a modified Soyuz, practicing rendezvous and docking techniques, and extending the duration of missions to 2½ weeks, which was accomplished in June, 1970 by Soyuz 9. Soyuz 10 was the first to dock with the Salyut 1 space station, on April 24, 1971, but some undisclosed technical problem prevented the three cosmonauts from boarding the station and the mission ended prematurely.

Soyuz 11 in June, 1971 got off to a more successful start. Georgi Dobrovolski, Viktor Patsayev and Vladislav Volkov spent 23 days in space aboard Salyut 1, at that time a record (the Apollo moon missions were still in progress, and Skylab had not yet been launched). But prior to re-entry, the air escaped from their Soyuz descent craft because of a leaky valve. The Soyuz touched down automatically on earth, but the recovery team found the crew dead in their seats. For the second time, a fatal tragedy had struck Soyuz.

Above: spider Arabella adapts to spinning its web in the zero-gravity conditions of Skylab.

Below: comet Kohoutek photographed streaking through space by Skylab during December 1973.

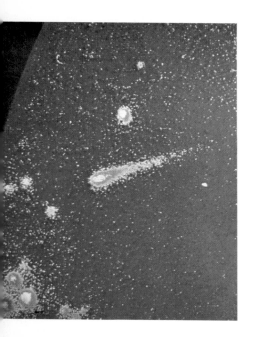

Soyuz flights were halted for two years while the craft was redesigned. The three Soyuz 11 cosmonauts had perished because they did not wear spacesuits; Soyuz was so small that there was no room for three men to do so. Henceforth, the Soyuz crew was reduced to two, wearing spacesuits.

Even the Salyut stations themselves were not immune from disaster. One Salyut was destroyed by a launch failure in July, 1972. Salyut 2, launched in April, 1973, broke up in orbit before it could be occupied. Another Salyut, launched a month after Salyut 2 in a rush to upstage Skylab, malfunctioned immediately on reaching orbit. The Russians never released further details about the mission.

Space station visits eventually resumed with Salyut 3 in 1974—but by then, American astronauts had completed their three outstanding missions aboard Skylab. In a field where they had once intended to be first, the U.S.S.R. had a lot of catching up to do. To make matters worse, they had a continuing series of irritating failures with their automatic docking mechanisms on Soyuz. And on April 5, 1975, a manned Soyuz capsule failed to orbit when the launch rocket malfunctioned; the cosmonauts returned to earth safely after a rough ride.

Politically, the most significant space event of this time was the Apollo-Soyuz Test Project (ASTP), a joint mission in orbit between an

Right: Soviet Soyuz spacecraft photographed from an American Apollo craft. Left to right, the photograph shows the cylindrical instrument module, the bell-shaped descent vehicle and the spherical orbital module.

Astronauts Thomas Stafford and Donald Slayton with the visiting cosmonaut Alexei Leonov in the Orbital Module of Soyuz 19.

American Apollo craft and a Russian Soyuz to demonstrate the prevailing spirit of detente—and to practice techniques for possible space rescue missions. The technical problems were many. For one thing, the two craft used different atmospheres. Apollo had an atmosphere of pure oxygen at low pressure; Soyuz used normal earth air at sea-level pressure. Each craft also had a different docking mechanism. To overcome these difficulties, Apollo carried with it into orbit a docking tunnel, which also served as an airlock between the spacecraft once they had joined up in orbit.

There was an extraordinary spirit of cooperation about ASTP, at least partly because neither side could afford an embarrassing failure. Spacemen and ground crews from both sides trained together, visited each other's space centers, and learned each other's languages. Some American politicians voiced doubts about the wisdom of the project

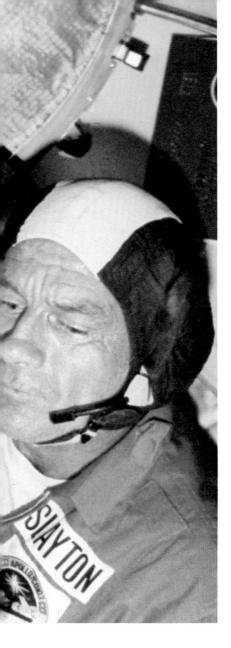

because of the poor Soyuz safety record. But the Russians flew a rehearsal mission and even had a second rocket standing by on launch day to allay the fears which they themselves also must have felt.

On July 15, 1975, Soyuz 19 carrying Alexei Leonov, the world's first space walker, and Valeri Kubasov, successfully climbed into orbit from the Russian cosmodrome near the town of Tyuratam northeast of the Aral Sea. Some hours later, Apollo carrying Tom Stafford, Vance Brand, and Donald Slayton left from Cape Canaveral to catch up and dock with Soyuz. The two craft remained linked for two days while the spacemen visited each other and carried out joint experiments. Then the two craft separated and landed in their normal recovery areas. For NASA, the mission was particularly poignant because it was the last flight of an Apollo. No more American astronauts would travel in space until the first launch of the Space Shuttle. It was a dramatically neat twist that Apollo, which had been conceived in the heat of political rivalry with the U.S.S.R., should have made its last flight jointly with a Russian spacecraft.

While the United States concentrated on developing its Space Shuttle, the Soviet Salyut program got firmly into its stride, eventually producing results that dwarfed even those of Skylab. Salyut's purposes were much the same as the American space station's—astronomical and geophysical observations, biological studies, and materials processing. In 1975, Pyotr Klimuk and Vitali Sevastyanov set a new Russian record by completing a 64-day mission aboard Salyut 4. These early Salyuts were only development models with short lifetimes, and they had to be regularly replaced. Salyut 5, like the earlier Salyut 3, is believed to have been used largely for military reconnaissance. Although two crews boarded it, no new records were set.

A new phase of Soviet space station missions began with the improved Salyut 6, launched on September 29, 1977. Unlike its predecessors, Salyut 6 had two docking ports, one at each end, so that it could be regularly resupplied by unmanned ferry craft and receive visiting cosmonauts while already occupied by a crew. This resupply facility allowed cosmonauts to stay aboard Salyut 6 for unprecedented lengths of time, building up unique experience in adaptation to weightlessness.

On December 10, 1977, Yuri Romanenko and Georgi Grechko took off in Soyuz 26 for what turned out to be a record-breaking 96-day flight aboard Salyut 6, surpassing even the milestone of the final Skylab flight. Their mission was marked by the start of visits by crews that included

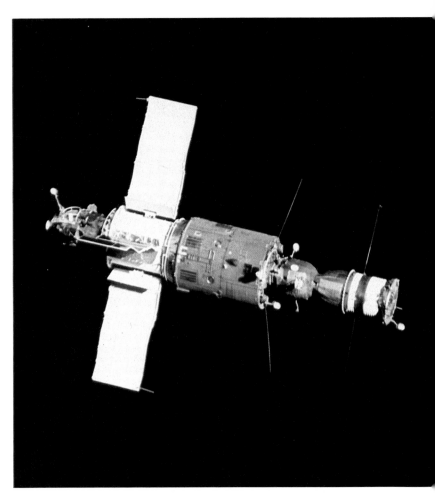

cosmonauts from other Communist countries. Vladimir Remek, a Czech air force pilot, became the first when he and Russian cosmonaut Alexei Gubarev visited Salyut 6 for a week in March, 1978.

Once the results of Romanenko and Grechko's long-duration flight had been digested, cosmonauts Vladimir Kovalyonok and Alexander Ivanchenkov set off on June 15, 1978, for a 140-day mission aboard Salyut 6. During their stay they were visited by more international crews including cosmonauts from Poland and East Germany.

Regular exercise ensured that the effects of long-term weightlessness, such as weakening of the heart and other muscles and loss of bone calcium, did not build up to dangerous levels. In fact, on their return to earth the cosmonauts were able to walk unaided from their Soyuz capsule. Kovalyonok and Ivanchenkov both readapted fully to normal earth gravity within ten days.

This augured well for even longer flights. The next step was taken by Vladimir Lyakhov and Valeri Ryumin who left earth on February 25, 1979, for a 175-day stay aboard Salyut 6. One of their first tasks was to replace worn-out equipment in the space station. Lyakhov and Ryumin had to endure their extended mission alone. An intended docking by Soyuz 33, containing a Bulgarian cosmonaut, Georgi Ivanov, was

Above left: Soyuz 28 on the launching pad at the Soviet Baikonur Cosmodrome, with its great retaining arms drawn back ready for liftoff.

Above right: the Soyuz/Salyut complex photographed in space from a visiting Soyuz craft.

cancelled because of a malfunction of the Soyuz maneuvering engine, and the disappointed crew had to make an emergency landing. Other planned visits by international crews were subsequently scratched while the problem was investigated. But automatic resupply ships brought up new provisions and equipment, including a 30-foot diameter radio telescope dish which was pushed out through an airlock and opened like an umbrella. The radio telescope was operated in conjunction with another dish on the ground to make observations of selected celestial objects.

Thanks to increased exercise during their flight, Lyakhov and Ryumin returned to earth in good health and actually readapted more quickly to normal gravity than had the previous record-breaking crew.

When a crew member for the next flight was injured during training, Ryumin offered to take his place. Realizing that this provided a unique opportunity to study man's long-term adaptation to space, Russian flight controllers accepted the offer. So it was that Valeri Ryumin and Leonid Popov spent 185 days aboard Salyut 6 during 1980, bringing Ryumin's total time in space to nearly a year.

Visitors this time were numerous and varied. They included a Hungarian, Bertalan Farkas; a Vietnamese, Pham Tuan; and a Cuban, Arnaldo Tamayo Mendez. Fittingly, the Cuban cosmonaut carried an experiment to study the effects of weightlessness on the crystallization of sugar, and part of the observational program for the Vietnamese was a survey of river silting in his home country. Other visitors were two cosmonauts on the maiden manned flight of an improved Soyuz, known as Soyuz T (the T stood for Transport). Soyuz T had room to ferry three cosmonauts into orbit.

One surprise from Popov and Ryumin's mission was that on their return to earth both cosmonauts were found to have put on weight, as distinct from all previous spacemen who had lost weight. This was hailed as a vindication of the varied diet and extensive exercise taken by the cosmonauts. On this evidence, there seemed no physical barrier to missions lasting a year or more, long enough for a trip to Mars.

Following the marathon missions in the Salyut 6 space station, Russian space controllers confidently predicted the establishment of permanent bases in orbit with interchangeable crews. These orbiting laboratories, they said, would be the forerunners of much larger space industrial factories which would have a major impact on technology, trade, and economics on earth.

The first international cosmonauts: Vladimir Remek (left) works aboard Salyut 6 with Russian Alexei Gubarev.

Working in the payload bay of Shuttle Orbiter *Atlantis* in November, 1985, Sherwood Spring and Jerry Ross demonstrate construction techniques that will be used to help assemble space station *Freedom* in the 1990's.

As a further step in this direction, the Soviet Union launched the improved Salyut 7 station in April, 1982. The following month Anatoli Berezovoi and Valentin Lebedev took up residence, and remained there until December. By staying in orbit for 211 days, they captured the space duration record. During their long sojurn in space, they were visited by several teams of cosmonauts. They included in June, 1982 the Frenchman Jean-Loup Chretien, who thus became the first western European to go into space. In August, 1982 the three-person crew of Soyuz T-7 to visit Salyut 7 included Svetlana Savitskaya. She was only the second woman ever to travel in space.

Salyut 7 continued to support long-stay missions, but was not without its problems. By the fall of 1983, the space station was suffering from propellant leakage and from an ailing electrical system. On September 27 cosmonauts Vladimir Titov and Gennadi Strekalov prepared to launch on a repair mission, but 90 seconds before liftoff their launch rocket exploded on the pad. But thanks to the launch escape system the two cosmonauts were rocketed away from the conflagration and landed unhurt two miles away.

On October 1, 1984 the space duration record fell once again, when three rather frail cosmonauts, Leonid Kizim, Vladimir Solovyov and Oleg Atkov, returned after remaining in orbit for nearly 237 days. Their visitors during this period had included in July Svetlana Savitskaya, returning to space for the second time and also making the first ever spacewalk by a woman. In so doing she upstaged American astronauts Sally Ride, who was about to make her second space trip, and Kathy Sullivan, who was about to make a spacewalk, both on Shuttle mission 41-G in October, 1984.

Kizim and Solovyov were also the first two cosmonauts to enter Salyut 7's successor, *Mir* (meaning peace), in March, 1986, a month after it had been launched. *Mir* is similar in design to the Salyuts but is outfitted mainly as an accommodation module. Scientific experiments take place in add-on modules, flown up by remote control. In *Mir*, cosmonauts Musa Manarov and Vladimir Titov on December 21, 1988, completed over a year in orbit.

In 1988 too United States President Ronald Reagan named the space station NASA is scheduled to build in the mid-1990's, *Freedom*. The station is being built as an international enterprise, with Europe, Canada and Japan making major contributions. *Freedom* will be permanently crewed by a team of six, who will work aloft in shifts of about three months at a time. The station will be constructed by the assembly of modules ferried up by Shuttles.

Up in orbit, a Shuttle Orbiter delivers another module for the space station as work nears completion in the last years of the 20th century. As many as 20 Shuttle missions will be required to ferry up materials and personnel to assemble the station.

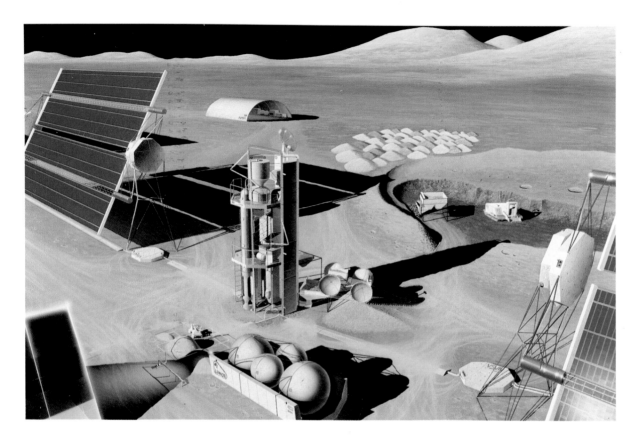

Above: looking beyond the space station and into the early years of the next century, the moon will once again become a major target for exploration. This time a permanent base will be set up, which will eventually become largely self-supporting. The picture shows a plant set up by a lunar colony to extract oxygen from the rocks.

Left: space station *Freedom*, how it might appear at the turn of the century. Huge panels of solar cells provide the electrical power. The cylindrical modules provide the living and working quarters for the scientists and engineers who make up the crew. Nearby is a free-flying platform, which can be tended by spacewalking service engineers.

The main part of the space station is made up of four modules of cylindrical shape. They are about 50 feet long and some 15 feet across, a size that fits the payload bay of the Shuttle Orbiter. The modules are interconnected by so-called resource nodes. NASA is in overall charge of space station construction and provides two of the modules, the habitation and American laboratory modules.

Two other laboratory modules are being supplied by the European Space Agency (ESA) and Japan. ESA is also contributing a free-flying remote-controlled facility and an instrument-carrying platform to operate away from the station in polar orbit. Canada is supplying a mobile servicing system, which is able to move around the space station structure to assist the loading and unloading of visiting Shuttles, assist satellite servicing, and so on. For their design, the Canadians are drawing on their experience in building the remote manipulator arm of the Shuttle, which has proved extremely versatile.

When *Freedom* becomes fully operational, resident astronaut-engineers will take over the satellite-recovery and servicing duties which Shuttle astronauts currently carry out. Satellites in high orbits will be recovered using a kind of space tug called the orbital maneuvering vehicle (OMV), operated remotely from the station.

The establishment of a permanent space station will have a profound effect on future space exploration. It will eventually act as a construction base for the assembly of lunar and interplanetary spacecraft, which will lead to manned bases being set up first on the moon and then on Mars, even to colonies floating in space (see page 171).

The Shuttle Era
10

Welcome aboard for the flight of your life! One day you could experience the miracle of space flight, without becoming a highly trained astronaut of the old school. No longer do you need to be a daredevil test pilot with thousands of hours of jet flight experience. No longer do you need to fly into space in a bulky spacesuit.

The new revolution in space travel has been wrought by the American Space Shuttle, a regular "truck service" into orbit and back again for men and materials. The key to the Shuttle system is that it is reusable. In all previous US manned space flights, the main rocket was destroyed after doing its job of launching the spacecraft into orbit, and even if a part of the spacecraft returned to earth, it was not fit for reuse. However, in the Space Shuttle system, the two launch (booster) rockets parachute back to earth, to be recovered and used again. And the winged spacecraft, the Space Shuttle Orbiter, returns to earth, gliding down through the atmosphere to land on a runway.

The Shuttle Orbiter is a delta-winged craft the size of a DC9 jet airliner, 122 feet long and with a wingspan of 78 feet. The main part of the Orbiter's body is made up of a payload (cargo) bay, 60 feet long, capable of carrying up to about 25 tons into orbit and bringing back 14 tons to earth.

A major payload of the Shuttle is the European-developed space laboratory (Spacelab). And the time is approaching when a university researcher will be able to suggest an experiment and actually fly into space along with it. You'll still have to be a pretty extraordinary sort of person—but, after about a year of testing and training, it could be your turn to ride into the future. You would fly as a payload specialist and be responsible for the operation of one of the experimental payloads on board.

The Orbiter's cabin has three storeys—an upper flight deck, a living area on the mid-deck, and a lower deck filled with equipment. The Orbiter carries a crew of up to seven people, both men and women. The astronauts who actually fly the craft are the commander and the pilot. They are more like the early astronauts in that they are skilled pilots with hundreds of hours of high-speed flight experience. The remainder of the crew are either mission specialists or payload specialists. The mission specialists are professional astronauts, usually scientists and engineers, who are highly trained in all aspects of Shuttle and payload operations except for piloting the craft. They are responsible for the smooth running of each flight and handle operations like launching satellites. The payload specialists again are scientists or

The world's first "space truck," the Space Shuttle Orbiter *Columbia*, sits on the launch pad at Cape Canaveral, Florida, prior to its maiden flight into orbit in April, 1981. It is mated to a large external fuel tank and two solid-propellant booster rockets.

engineers, who fly with a particular payload, and who will probably fly into space only the once.

The flight deck seats four, so if you are lucky, you'll be able to sit on the flight deck while the remainder of the crew sit on the mid-deck. As you step onto the flight deck you will see the four seats: two in front for the commander and pilot, and two behind, one for a mission specialist, and one for you.

The flight deck looks very like its counterpart on a conventional

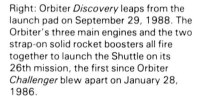

Right: Orbiter *Discovery* leaps from the launch pad on September 29, 1988. The Orbiter's three main engines and the two strap-on solid rocket boosters all fire together to launch the Shuttle on its 26th mission, the first since Orbiter *Challenger* blew apart on January 28, 1986.

Left: the Orbiter's remote manipulator arm, the Shuttle's crane, plucks a satellite from the payload bay and places it in orbit. The crane has proved an invaluable aid to spacewalking astronauts as well.

airliner, with banks of instruments and forward-facing windows. Peer over the commander's shoulder and you'll see three television screens displaying computer information; instruments showing airspeed, altitude and direction; caution and warning lights—and the instruments for flying the Shuttle. These consist of a pistol-grip steering column, rudder pedals and an air-brake lever. The instruments are duplicated for the pilot in much the same way as in an airliner.

There'll be one big difference from an airliner: after you've climbed into your seat, you'll be lying on your back looking through the windows at the sky. The Shuttle goes straight up during launching.

For launch, the Shuttle Orbiter is mated to a fuel tank which feeds liquid hydrogen and liquid oxygen to the Orbiter's cluster of three main engines. At the sides of the fuel tank are attached two solid-fuel booster rockets (SRBs). All engines fire at liftoff, giving a total thrust of nearly 3,000 tons, compared with the 3,400 tons thrust of a Saturn V. On the launch pad, the overall Shuttle system stands 184 feet tall and weighs 2,000 tons.

All is ready as the seconds are counted out for launching. There is a roar and a shudder as the Orbiter's liquid-fueled engines jump into life, followed by its two solid boosters. Slowly the Shuttle starts to rise, and your body weight builds up to three times its normal earth value— uncomfortable, but not painful.

At an altitude of 27 miles the solid-fuel boosters fall away, parachuting into the ocean where they are recovered for reuse, leaving the Orbiter's own main engines to power it toward orbit about 200 miles above the earth. Shortly before reaching orbit, the external fuel tank falls away and burns up in the atmosphere; it is the only part of the system not scheduled for reuse. Then the two orbital maneuvering system engines in the tail fire briefly to nudge the Orbiter into orbit. In only about 10 minutes the Shuttle's mighty rockets have thrust you from the launch pad into orbit, circling the earth at 17,500 mph.

Below: scientists absorbed in their work during the first Spacelab flight in November, 1983 in Orbiter *Columbia*, making its sixth trip into space. On the left is the West German Ulf Merbold, the first European to fly on an American spacecraft. In the background is fellow payload specialist Byron Lichtenberg. On the right is mission specialist Robert Parker. They worked in alternate shifts with the remaining three crew members.

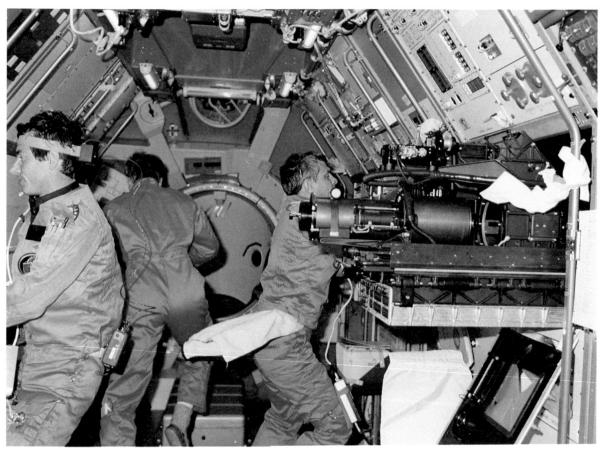

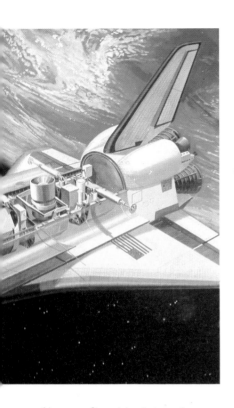

Above: on Spacelab missions, the space laboratory remains inside the open payload bay of the Shuttle Orbiter. The scientists work inside a pressurized laboratory module, which has state-of-the-art equipment and its own computing facilities. A separate unpressurized pallet carries instruments that need to be exposed to the space environment.

Up in orbit, with the engines switched off, thrust and vibrations cease. You are now weightless. Blood rushes to your head, making your face puffy and your nose stuffy. You unstrap yourself and float gently through the hatch into Spacelab, where you and your fellow scientists will be working 12-hour shifts for the next week. Your duties might include taking photographs of the earth and sky with special cameras and telescopes, operating a furnace for processing materials, and observing under a microscope the behavior of cells in weightlessness. You may also be a guinea pig yourself for experiments on the adaptation of humans to their first space flight.

Spacelab stays in the Orbiter's cargo bay. There are two main parts to Spacelab: a pressurized workshop in which scientists carry out experiments, and pallets open to space on which equipment is mounted. Spacelab can be flown with just the pressurized module or with pallets alone, but a typical mission will use both. The pressurized section is about 13 feet in diameter, and is usually about 23 feet long. Spacelab scientists are continuing the experiments on space processing of materials begun by Skylab astronauts. Other Skylab tasks include studying the earth's landforms, oceans and atmosphere, biological and medical experiments and astronomical observations.

The first Spacelab flight took place on November 28, 1983. The Orbiter *Columbia* carried the space laboratory into orbit on its sixth mission. The flight was notable because one of the two payload specialists on board was the West German scientist Ulf Merbold. He became the first non-American to fly in an American spacecraft. The commander of the mission, John Young, also set a record, for he was making his sixth space flight. The six Spacelab astronauts worked around the clock in three-man shifts, carrying out over 70 experiments. The mission was an outstanding success and was extended to 10 days to give extra working time.

The next three Spacelab missions all took place in 1985. On April 29 came the Spacelab 3 mission (actually number 2), which carried into space a mini-zoo of two squirrel monkeys and 24 rats. One interesting bonus for this mission was the observation of a magnificent display of the Northern lights, which had never been seen from space before. The flight was also interesting because three of the crew were aged over 50, William Thornton being 56. This emphasized the user-friendly nature of the Shuttle, and showed that age was no longer a barrier to space flight. The Spacelab 2 mission in July carried only instruments, while the third mission of the year, in October, saw Spacelab devoted to experiments by West Germany, who funded the flight.

Above: on the mid-deck of Orbiter *Challenger* a maximum crew of seven pose topsy turvily for the camera on the 51-F Shuttle mission in August, 1985. They are, clockwise from top right: Gordon Fullerton, Anthony England, Karl Henize, Roy Bridges, Loren Acton and John-David Bartoe. In the center is Story Musgrave.

When not at work in Spacelab you'll be in the Orbiter's living area on the mid-deck, where there are sleeping bunks, a galley, and bathroom with a special toilet designed to work in zero gravity.

Mealtimes will be a treat—in stark contrast to the experiences of early astronauts who complained bitterly of lukewarm food squeezed from tubes and dehydrated food reconstituted with hot water. The Space Shuttle has a galley area with a battery of kitchen equipment that could stand comparison with the most modern American kitchen. It takes about 30 minutes to prepare a meal. The various foods are stored together in individual containers. Most of the foods are dehydrated and are prepared by squirting water into their containers. Other foods are canned or in their natural form. The astronauts take turn to be "chef of the day," placing the appropriate containers in the oven of the galley unit when they need heating, and assembling the other foods on individual trays for each astronaut. The astronauts eat with ordinary cutlery, although they must be careful not to make jerky movements which would dislodge the food. Liquids are drunk not from a glass—liquids cannot pour in weightlessness—but by sucking with a straw.

Menus are planned to give you 3,000 calories a day. There are 74 kinds of food, which can give six days' menu without repetition. If you don't like a particular dish you can select an alternative. Items on the menu include scrambled eggs and sausage for breakfast; mushroom

Left: mission specialist Guion Bluford takes a turn on the Shuttle treadmill exercise device. He wears an elasticated harness to keep his feet on the floor, otherwise he would bounce up to the ceiling every step.

soup and cheese sandwiches for lunch; and shrimp cocktail with steak and strawberries for dinner.

After such a sumptuous meal, perhaps a little exercise is called for! Shuttle astronauts take their exercise on a treadmill on the mid-deck. This helps keep their muscles in tone. Shuttle flights are not long enough for any serious deterioration to take place in the muscles—this happens on extended flights like those on space stations like *Mir*.

Among the most welcome modern conveniences on the Shuttle is the flushing toilet. This does away with the old practice of using plastic bags to deal with what NASA delicately calls "digestive elimination." The Shuttle toilet does not look too different from its counterpart on earth, but it does have a few unearthly features, including foot-rests and a seat-belt! The flushing is done, not by water, as on earth, but by a stream of air. The urine is drawn separately into a hose and eventually dumped overboard. Solid wastes are drawn onto a fan, which shreds and flings them onto the walls of a lower chamber, where they are freeze-dried and taken back for disposal on earth.

Shuttle astronauts are not so lucky as the Skylab astronauts because they do not have a shower—there is no room. They have to be content with a sponge-down wash. There is no shortage of water on the Shuttle, incidentally. It is produced as a by-product from the fuel cells that generate the on-board electricity.

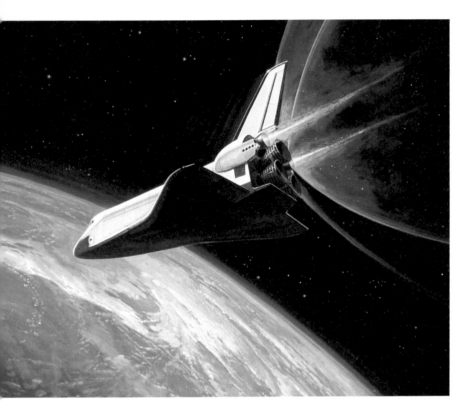

Above: re-entry. The Orbiter is turned so that it is moving tail-first, and two small on-board engines are fired to slow it down. Gravity then pulls it back into the atmosphere.

All too soon, your week in space is at an end. Reluctantly, you close the hatch to Spacelab and take your seat for re-entry. Above the Pacific Ocean, maneuvering rockets are fired to push the Orbiter back into the earth's atmosphere. Insulating tiles made of silica and carbon on the Shuttle's nose, wings and underside protect it from the heat of re-entry. Following your prolonged spell of weightlessness you feel as though you are being crushed into your seat, although re-entry forces are kept to about 1½ G's. Half an hour after re-entry began you are approaching the runway at Edwards Air Force Base in California, where Spacelab flights always terminate.

The astronauts, with the considerable assistance of an impressive array of electronic gadgetry, pilot the Shuttle down to land on the long runway. There is one major difference between the Shuttle's landing and that of an aircraft: the Shuttle's engines do not operate during descent, so in the atmosphere it functions purely as a glider.

Several jarring bumps tell you the Shuttle is back on earth again. Cautiously you stretch your legs under the burden of earth gravity, and disembark to begin the analysis of your results. Meanwhile the Orbiter will be flown by jumbo jet back to the Kennedy Space Center, where it will be prepared for another launch in a few months' time.

Probably on the next launch the Orbiter will be used to launch one or more satellites, its usual payload. Or it may be scheduled for a satellite recovery and repair mission. Spacewalking Shuttle astronauts have already proved how versatile they can be in this direction.

Since the Orbiter enters only a low orbit around the earth, payloads destined for higher orbit, such as geostationary satellites, or space

probes which will leave the earth altogether, must have an additional rocket stage attached, which is fired once it is well clear of the Shuttle.

Any organization, such as a university or an industrial concern, can buy payload space aboard the Shuttle much as though it were a normal cargo plane. Of particular interest to small organizations are the so-called Getaway Specials, self-contained payloads weighing 60 to 200 pounds which can be squeezed into spare corners of the cargo bay at low cost.

The Kennedy Space Center, the world's premier spaceport, is the main launch site of the Shuttle. It lies just inland from Cape Canaveral, a few miles from where the pioneering Mercury astronauts led the United States into the space age. The launch facilities at the so-called Complex 39 have been much modified from those used by the Apollo program. In the giant Vehicle Assembly Building, Shuttle Orbiters are mated to their fuel tank and booster rockets, and are rolled out on the same crawler transporters to the launch pads from which Saturn V rockets departed for the moon.

A runway has been added for returning Shuttle Orbiters, but only a few landings have taken place there. The weather has proved notoriously unreliable. Most flights in fact have terminated at the Edwards Air Force Base in the Mojave Desert in California. There the runway is extremely long and allows plenty of room for the Orbiters to overshoot if need be. Launch facilities have also been built for the Shuttle at the Vandenberg Air Force Base in California, where it can be launched on military and polar missions. But no flights had taken place there by 1989.

Above: just a few feet above the runway, Orbiter *Discovery* comes in to land at Edwards Air Force Base in California on September 5, 1984. It has just completed its 6-day maiden flight, with complete success. It carries the second American spacewoman, Judy Resnik, who will later perish in the *Challenger* disaster attempting her second flight.

Right: a dramatic low-angle photograph captures Orbiter *Atlantis* a few seconds after it has blasted loose from the launch pad on October 3, 1985. It is about to make its maiden voyage into space. The mission, 51-J, carries a secret Department of Defense payload. With *Atlantis* now operational, the Shuttle fleet is at full strength.

Work on the Space Shuttle began in 1970, and the present design was chosen two years later. Construction of a prototype Orbiter named *Enterprise* was completed in 1977, when it was test flown in the atmosphere. In these so-called approach and landing tests, conducted between August and October 1977, *Enterprise* was carried aloft on the back of a converted jumbo jet and then released to be piloted back to the ground by its two astronauts.

Enterprise, named after the spaceship commanded by Captain Kirk in the TV series Star Trek, could never fly into space because it lacked real engines and heat insulating tiles. Following its atmospheric flights, it was taken to the Kennedy Space Center, where it was used to rehearse launch procedures. After these were completed it was stripped down to provide spare parts for other Orbiters, four of which were initially built: *Columbia*, *Challenger*, *Discovery* and *Atlantis*.

Columbia should have made its space début in 1979, but problems with the heat-shield tiles and the main engines caused a two-year delay. It finally thundered into space on April 12, 1981, 20 years to the day since Yuri Gagarin blazed the astronaut trail into orbit. *Columbia* completed a flawless mission a little over two days later, piloted by space veteran John Young and rookie Robert Crippen.

The pioneering Orbiter was back on the launch pad just seven months later, poised for its second space flight. On November 12, *Columbia* again took to the skies, and became the first ever spacecraft to return to space. Over the next year *Columbia* repeated this feat three times more, and on its fifth flight became officially operational and carried into orbit two communications satellites. Its sister ship *Challenger* made its space début on April 4, 1983, *Discovery* followed on August 30, 1984, and *Atlantis* on October 30, 1985. But the Shuttle fleet was at full strength for only a few weeks.

On January 28, 1986, *Challenger* lifted off the launch pad on the 25th Shuttle mission, but after 73 seconds was blasted apart by a gigantic explosion. The seven astronaut crew perished in the fireball that ensued. This postponed Shuttle flights for two-and-a-half years, while many design changes were made to the main engines, and the solid rocket boosters, together with other Shuttle systems and operating procedures. Particular attention was paid to the redesign of the boosters to prevent the failure that had led to the *Challenger* tragedy. Shuttle flights resumed when *Discovery* soared into the heavens on September 29, 1988, and completed a flawless mission. A new Shuttle Orbiter, named *Endeavour*, is currently being built, and is scheduled for a maiden flight in 1992.

Above: NASA's first attempt at satellite recovery took place in April, 1984. The satellite, Solar Max, is eventually snared by the remote manipulator arm, visible on the right. It is shown secured in the payload bay, ready for repair.

Unlike early astronauts, who wore spacesuits for most of the time they spent in space, Shuttle astronauts live and work in shirt-sleeve comfort. The Shuttle Orbiter is pressurized with a nitrogen/oxygen mixture just like air, and at ordinary earth sea-level pressure. Only when the astronauts leave their craft to go on EVA do they need to wear spacesuits. EVA means extravehicular activity; the popular name for it is spacewalking.

The Shuttle spacesuit, or EMU (extravehicular mobility unit) is made up of two parts, upper torso and trousers. The two parts seal around the waist. The suit is made up of many layers, which serve to protect the astronaut from the deadly space environment. Beneath the suit the astronaut wears a pair of long-johns, water cooled to keep him or her at a comfortable temperature. A backpack built into the upper part of the suit houses the portable life-support system, which provides oxygen for breathing, water for body cooling and electrical power.

When performing tasks in orbit, the astronaut dons a Buck Rogers-style, jet-propelled backpack, called the MMU, or manned maneuvering unit. This unit has sets of small jet thrusters dotted all around it. By means of controls on the arms, an astronaut can fire the thrusters to travel in any direction. Bruce McCandless flight-tested the

MMU for the first time on February 7, 1984, becoming the first human satellite.

The first operational use of the MMU came on mission 41-C in April, 1984, when George Nelson flew over to the ailing satellite Solar Max and attempted to dock with it. He was not successful. But fortunately the satellite was later retrieved with the help of Orbiter *Challenger*'s remote manipulator arm, operated from inside by Terry Hart. After Solar Max had been securely stowed in the payload bay, James van Hoften and George Nelson deftly removed faulty equipment modules and installed new ones. The repairs proved entirely successful, and after re-launch Solar Max once again began feeding data about activity on the sun to ground control.

Only seven months afterwards, Orbiter *Discovery* blasted off to attempt an even more challenging mission, the capture of two communications satellites, Westar VI and Palapa B2, which had failed immediately after deployment on mission 41-B the previous February. The plan was for astronauts flying MMUs to fix a gadget called a stinger in each satellite, and fly back with it to the Orbiter. The satellites would then be stowed in the payload bay and returned to earth, where repairs could be undertaken.

Above: during Shuttle mission 51-A, on one of the most exciting spacewalks ever attempted, Dale Gardner fixes a ''stinger'' to the Westar communications satellite prior to jetting back with it to Orbiter *Discovery*. He is wearing and flying the MMU.

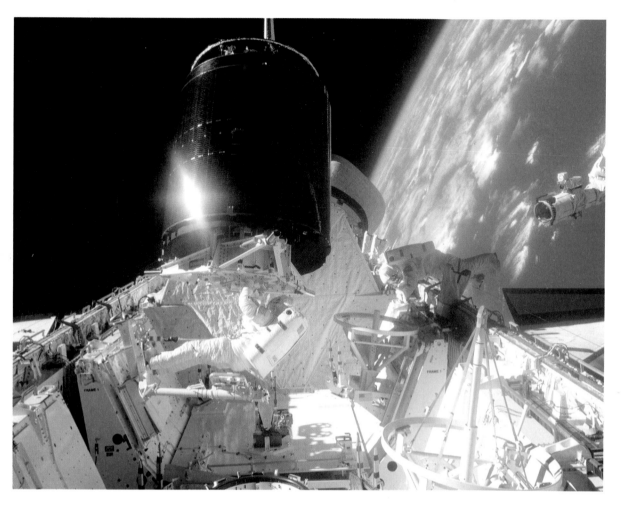

Above: wrestling with one of the captured communications satellites on Shuttle mission 51-A, Dale Gardner awaits the assistance of fellow spacewalker Joseph Allen. The stingers they used to capture the satellites are stowed on the right.

The operation went like a dream. First Joseph Allen flew over to Palapa, secured the stinger, and flew back to Dale Gardner waiting in the payload bay. Together they manhandled the satellite into clamps in the bay. Next it was Gardner's turn to fly the stinger over to Westar and back to Allen, again with complete success. Within days the errant satellites, worth about $150 million, were back on the ground. Lloyds, Britain's premier insurance company, were especially delighted. They had paid out the insurance money on the satellites! Now they could make good their losses.

Two missions later, 51-D in April, 1985, *Discovery* was aloft on a routine satellite launch operation. But one of the launches did not go as planned. The satellite Leasat 3 refused to work after it had been deployed. The occasion was embarrassing to say the least because on board was Senator Jake Garn, who was a member of the committee that determined the NASA budget!

So, for the first time in the Shuttle era, an unscheduled spacewalk took place to try to activate the dead satellite. Jeffrey Hoffman and David Griggs went out into the payload bay and attached an ingenious makeshift "flyswatter" to the remote manipulator arm. Then Rhea Seddon attempted to flick a switch on the satellite with the flyswatter,

ЭНЕРГИЯ

СССР

but without success. The attempts to activate the satellite were not without danger, for had its booster rocket suddenly fired the Orbiter and the crew could have been lost.

Discovery returned home empty and suffered the further ignominy of getting a flat tire on landing. NASA decided to mount another recovery mission and attempt to repair Leasat in orbit. This mission, 51-I, in August, 1985, saw James van Hoften, nicknamed "the Ox" because of his strength, grab Leasat and help stow it in the payload bay. Fellow spacewalker William Fisher (whose wife Anna is also an astronaut) carried out the necessary repairs before the Ox relaunched Leasat again, by hand. Before long, Leasat was working.

The final spacewalk of 1985, on mission 41-B in November with Orbiter *Atlantis*, was equally spectacular. Sherwood Spring and Jerry Ross were involved this time, rehearsing construction techniques that will be used in the construction of NASA's international space station in the mid-1990's. The two astronauts practiced assembling interlinking beams and struts of two different designs, called EASE (experimental assembly of structures in extravehicular activity) and ACCESS (assembly concept for construction of erectable space structures). They found the work easier than expected.

Above: ready on the launch pad in November, 1988 is the Soviet shuttle craft *Buran*. It is mounted atop the most powerful rocket in existence, Energia. Liftoff took place on November 15, and the mission lasted 3½ hours.

Is there Life out There?
11

Far out in the reaches of our solar system a message from earth is being sent into space. For billions of years it will wander through the universe like a message in a bottle, waiting for the remote chance of discovery.

The message is a gold-anodized aluminum plate, six inches by nine inches, attached to the antenna support struts of Pioneer 10, the American space probe designed to take a close look at Jupiter and Saturn before disappearing into the vastness of space. The picture etched on the plaque is difficult for the layman to understand—apart from two naked figures of a man and a woman. But the man who helped to design it, American astronomer Carl Sagan, says in his book *The Cosmic Connection* that it is intended to communicate the locale, epoch, and something of the nature of the builders of the spacecraft. "It is written in the only language we share with the recipients: science." Just who those "recipients" might be no one can say. The message on Pioneer 10 was added at the last minute in the faint, very faint, hope that someone, or something, will one day find the space probe—and know that back here on earth there are, or were, thinking, intelligent life forms.

Since then three more messages have gone out on space probes: an identical plaque on Pioneer's twin, Pioneer 11; and long-playing records containing sound effects on earth and greetings in various languages placed aboard Voyagers 1 and 2. All four messages will eventually leave our solar system for deep space, where they will drift on for ever. The expected erosion rate in interstellar space is so slow that the messages should remain intact for hundreds of millions of years. Which is just as well. Pioneer 10 is not expected to enter the planetary system of any star we can see from earth for at least 10 billion years.

The decision to include these messages on the space probes was taken in the belief, indeed the hope, that we are not alone in the universe. As Sagan put it, "There may be a time when contact will be made with another intelligence on a planet of some far-distant star, beings with millions of years of quite independent evolution, beings with no prospect of looking very much like us—although they may think very much like us."

Jupiter and its four largest satellites, Io, Europa, Ganymede and Callisto. This is a montage of Voyager space probe pictures.

Above: a Pioneer Venus blasts off from Cape Canaveral in 1978.

Below: the Pioneer Venus probe photographed the changing cloud patterns of Venus. These two pictures were taken 16 days apart.

What are the chances of life out there? In 1961 a symposium of scientists meeting at America's National Radio Astronomy Observatory at Green Bank, West Virginia, decided that there might be between 10,000 and 1,000 million civilizations in our galaxy alone. The earth is just one of nine planets which revolve around the sun. The sun is just one of 100,000 million stars in the Milky Way. And there are more galaxies in the universe than there are stars in the Milky Way. Faced with the infinity of space, the real surprise would be to discover that mankind is alone in the universe.

Isaac Asimov, the American biochemist and space specialist, uses a technique based on deductive logic, the best evidence available, and current theories to reach a figure of 530,000 technological civilizations now in being. He concentrates exclusively on the number of civilizations in our galaxy because the Milky Way itself measures 100,000 light years in diameter, and the other galaxies are so awesomely distant that, with the technology man has been able to develop, it would be impossible to contact them. Most scientists agree, then, that there must be life out there. The question is: how do we find it?

Neil Armstrong's moon trip ended forever speculation about civilizations on our companion in space. He found no water on the moon—and no air. And most scientists agree that there can be no life in a world without some kind of atmosphere, and some kind of liquid.

If not on the moon, where then? Our knowledge of the solar system has increased by space leaps and bounds during the past 20 years—thanks mainly to the work of long-range space probes, which have

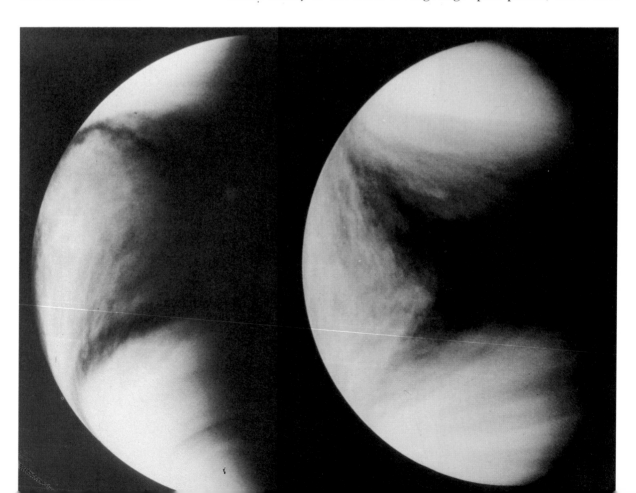

photographed and even landed on the nearest of our planets.

Venus comes closer to earth than any other planet—24 million miles at its nearest—but both Russian and American probes have shown it to be the nearest place to Hell.

Poisonous carbon dioxide envelops the planet, sealing in a furnace-like temperature of nearly 900°F (475°C). Any life form on Venus would have to find a way of resisting atmospheric pressure nearly 90 times that at the surface of the earth. If such a life form did manage to overcome that problem, it would live on a surface strewn with rocks—according to photographs taken from the surface of Venus by Venus 9 and 10 in 1975. The boulders are scoured into weird shapes by constant dust storms and nothing can grow in the stifling heat.

Venus is almost as big as the earth, but rotates on its axis in the opposite direction. In December 1978, an American Pioneer probe went into orbit around Venus to map its hidden surface by radar. It built up a map of the planet showing what appear to be several continental areas, including a mountain higher than Everest and twin volcanoes larger than any on earth.

Also in December 1978, a cluster of five instrumented packages released by another Pioneer probe plunged into the atmosphere of Venus, measuring conditions from the cloud tops to the surface. They found that the clouds of Venus are made of concentrated sulphuric acid, stronger than in a car battery. They also registered flashes of lightning crackling incessantly through the acrid atmosphere.

If not Venus, what about the planet nearest to the sun, Mercury?

Below: part of a radar map of Venus sent back to earth by a Pioneer Venus space probe put into orbit in December 1978. The lowest areas are coloured blue, and the highest areas are yellow and brown. The large continent at top center is called Ishtar Terra, and is the size of Australia. Left of center is Beta Regio, composed of two large volcanoes. At right is Aphrodite Terra, half the size of Africa. Black areas were unmapped.

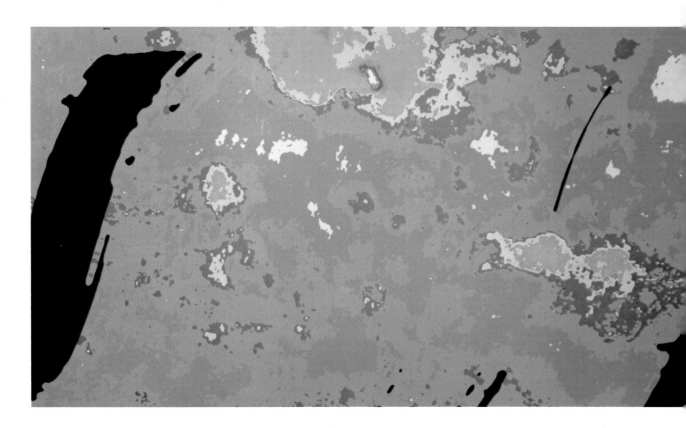

Right: Mars photographed by the Viking 2 probe during its approach to the red planet. A plume of cloud streams away from the peak of a Martian mountain, top center. At bottom, an ice field surrounds a crater. The Martian "grand canyon" is visible at center right.

Above: a model of Nix Olympica, a giant shield volcano on Mars, larger than the island of Hawaii. Nix Olympica is 375 miles wide and 15 miles high.

One of the most successful of the American probes, Mariner 10, passed 500 miles above the surface of Mercury in 1974. Mariner 10's pictures showed Mercury to be an airless, waterless and cratered body looking very much like our own moon. Evidently, the same bombardment of meteoroids which scarred the moon early in its history has also left its mark on Mercury.

Without an atmosphere, the planet is bathed in searing radiation from the sun. On its sunward face, the surface of Mercury heats up to 752°F (400°C), hot enough to melt tin and lead, whereas in the long Mercurian night, exposed to the frigid vacuum of space, temperatures drop to −283°F (−175°C).

Traveling away from the sun, out into the solar system, the first planet we would find is Mars, a world long believed to be the home of intelligent beings. Certainly, of all the planets on which life might arise, Mars has always seemed the most likely. It is also the next target for manned exploration. As seen through a telescope from earth, Mars appears as an orange-coloured ball with bright polar caps and smudgy dark markings. It spins on its axis in almost the same time as the earth does, although it is only half the size.

For much of this century, astronomers thought that the dark markings of Mars could be patches of vegetation. Some observers even believed they could see long, straight markings which they interpreted as canals, dug by Martians to bring water from the planet's poles to their crops in the red deserts. Alas, this notion has not survived investigation. Long before the first probes reached Mars it was realized that the planet's atmosphere was too thin, and the temperature too cold, for any advanced life.

Prospects of life receded further when America's Mariner 4 sent

Above: the surface of Mars viewed by the Viking 1 Lander. Mars resembles a rocky desert, colored strongly red by the presence of copious amounts of iron oxide.

Left: a model of the Viking Lander during tests on earth. A long arm stretches out to scoop up samples of the soil, while a radio dish sends back pictures and results to earth.

back the first close-up pictures of Mars in July 1965 showing the surface to be cratered, rather like the moon's. Five years later, Mariners 6 and 7 reinforced this view of a moon-like Mars. The dark areas turned out to be not vegetation after all, but areas of darker rock.

But up until then, only small areas of the planet had been photographed as probes flew past. The whole of Mars had yet to be mapped. That was the task of Mariner 9, which went into orbit around the red planet on November 13, 1971. Its pictures created a revolution in our understanding of Mars.

Mariner 9 photographed an enormous canyon, 2,500 miles long and up to 75 miles wide, similar in appearance to the rift valley in Africa.

There were volcanoes on Mars, the largest of which is 15 miles high and 375 miles wide, larger than any volcano on earth, including the Hawaiian islands. There were winding channels that looked like dried-up river beds, and other areas that appeared as though they had been flooded in the past, perhaps when the climate was warmer and wetter.

Although Mariner 9 found no evidence of life on Mars, its results showed that conditions in the past may have been suitable for life to arise. Perhaps that life, in the form of lowly plants or insects, clung to existence on the parched and frigid surface below. The only way to find out was to go down and look.

In the summer of 1976, two American Viking spacecraft arrived at Mars to search for life. Each Viking came in two halves: an orbiter which scanned the planet from above, and a lander which descended to the surface. In one of the greatest technical achievements of the space age, Viking 1 Lander touched down under control of its own computer brain on July 20, 1976.

Viking was festooned with instruments to measure the Martian soil and atmosphere. Soon after landing, Viking's TV eye opened to send the first views from the surface of Mars. They showed a red desert. Even the sky was pink, because of fine sand suspended in the thin air. The red color of the surface results from the presence in the rocks of considerable quantities of iron oxide, a substance familiar on earth as rust. A similar landscape was photographed by Viking 2 Lander when it touched down six weeks later on the other side of the planet in an area called Utopia.

Although rocks and sand dunes abounded on Mars, there was no sign of life. Viking's cameras would have spotted any insects hopping on the surface or burrowing in the soil, had they existed. But the absence of visible life did not rule out the possibility of microscopic

Winter frost forms white patches on the ground around the Viking 2 Lander on Mars in September 1977.

Voyager 2, targeted for Jupiter, Saturn and beyond, is launched from Cape Canaveral by Titan-Centaur rocket on August 20, 1977.

bugs. To test for such Martian micro-life, Viking carried a miniature biological laboratory.

First, Viking reached out its 10-foot long sampling arm to scoop up a handful of Martian soil, which it tipped gently into the experiment boxes. There, the soil was incubated in three different ways in an attempt to stimulate the growth of Martian micro-organisms. Nothing happened—and scientists believe, that without evidence to the contrary, there can be no life without organic compounds.

Beyond Mars, in the dark outer reaches of the solar system far from the sun, lie the giant planets Jupiter, Saturn, Uranus, and Neptune. Each of these is a ball of gas totally different in nature from the small, rocky inner planets such as the earth. The largest planet of all is Jupiter, 11 times the diameter of the earth, crossed by ever-changing bands of colored cloud. Jupiter's atmosphere contains only one permanent feature: an oval cloud known as the great red spot because of its size (large enough to swallow several earths) and its color.

Swirling cloud bands on Jupiter, seen by Voyager 1 from a distance of 12 million miles. In front of the planet are the orange moon Io, at left, and white-colored Europa, center right.

Pioneer 10 was launched on March 3, 1972, to make the first close-up survey of Jupiter, which it reached in December 1973, after a 21-month journey. It was followed a year later by an identical probe, Pioneer 11. The Pioneers found that Jupiter was surrounded by an extensive magnetic field with belts that contain deadly amounts of radiation. The probes confirmed that Jupiter is still cooling from the time of its birth, giving off $2\frac{1}{2}$ times as much heat as it receives from the sun. And their pictures showed the rising and falling convection currents that produce the belts and bands in Jupiter's atmosphere.

The Pioneers were pathfinders for an even more ambitious pair of spacecraft, called Voyager. Launched by the U.S.A. in the summer of 1977, Voyager 1 swept above Jupiter's cloud tops on March 5, 1979. Its twin followed four months later.

Their pictures showed swirling storms in Jupiter's atmosphere, with the red spot appearing as a hurricane-like vortex. But it was Jupiter's moons which created the biggest sensation. One moon, Io,

Jupiter's orange-and-red moon Io,
photographed in close-up by Voyager.
Io's color is produced by sulphur which
flows out from volcanoes dotted across
the moon's surface.

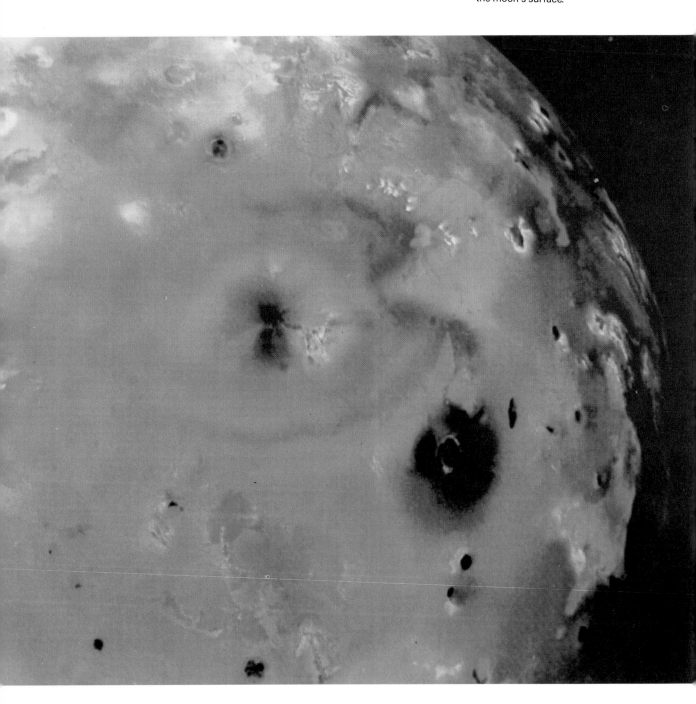

turned out to have an orange-colored surface coated with sulfur spewed out from active volcanoes, which Voyager photographed in the process of erupting. Another moon, Callisto, was saturated with impact craters, while the largest moon of all, Ganymede—bigger even than the planet Mercury—had a patchy surface of dark rock and bright ice fields, dotted with impact craters and scarred by strange grooves. A cracked icy crust enveloped the moon Europa. Among other surprises, a faint ring of dust particles was found around Jupiter, and lightning superbolts were seen in its stormy atmosphere.

Investigating Jupiter was only half the Voyagers' missions. The two probes then flew on to Saturn, revealing a host of new wonders. As Voyager 1 homed in on Saturn in November 1980, the rings, which seem so regular and continuous on cursory inspection from earth, broke up into as many as a thousand individual ringlets, like the grooves in a long-playing record. The rings are made up of ice-coated fragments of rock ranging in size from pebbles to house-size blocks.

The Voyagers also looked at Saturn's largest moon, Titan, 3,600 miles in diameter—large enough to be considered a planet in its own right— and the only moon in the solar system with a substantial atmosphere. Voyager found Titan's atmosphere to be made mostly of nitrogen, as is the earth's. Scientists now regard Titan as a primitive version of the earth, preserved in the deep freeze of the outer solar system. Unfortunately, Titan seems too cold for any form of life.

Voyager also discovered several new moons circling around Saturn, making at least 22 in all. Interestingly, some of these moons orbit close to some of the rings and appear to help keep the ring particles in place. They are appropriately known as shepherd moons.

Voyager 2 flew past Saturn in August, 1981, but its mission was not yet over. Accelerated by the "sling-shot" effect of the planet's gravity, it headed out for its next planetary rendezvous, with Uranus in January, 1986. Voyager 2 swooped within 50,000 miles of the cloud

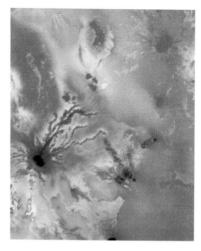

Above: flow of molten sulfur from a volcano on Io.

Right: turbulent streamers of cloud visible around Jupiter's great red spot, a gyrating storm three times the size of earth. In this Voyager picture, colors have been emphasized to show clouds at different levels. Near the red spot is an oval-shaped white cloud.

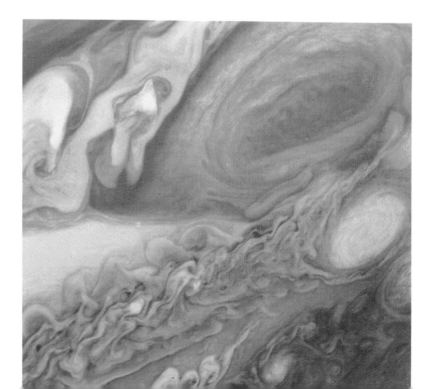

tops of Uranus on January 24. It showed the planet to have a greenish-blue atmosphere of hydrogen, helium and traces of methane. Below the atmosphere there is thought to be a vast hot ocean of water and ammonia, some 5,000 miles deep. Voyager also photographed the faint rings that surround the planet, which are only up to about 60 miles wide. They bear little resemblance to Saturn's glorious ring system, and are more like the faint one around Jupiter.

As it did at Saturn, Voyager discovered more new moons, including some that shepherd the ring particles. It took close-up pictures of the large moons of Uranus, Miranda, Ariel, Umbriel, Titania and Oberon. They all appear to be made up of rock and water ice. The most interesting moon by far is Miranda. It has a surface that is unique among moons in the solar system. In some areas the terrain changes abruptly from rolling plains to curious grooved regions, some of them oval in shape. Planetary geologists reckon that such features are the result of a violent collision the moon suffered in the distant past. They think that the collision shattered Miranda to pieces, and then the pieces eventually came together again under gravity to re-form the moon.

Exactly on schedule, on August 25, 1989, Voyager 2 swooped within 3,000 miles of the cloud tops of Neptune. At the time the planet was nearly 3 billion miles away from earth. The pictures the probe sent back showed Neptune to be a blue world, criss-crossed by bands of wispy clouds. It has a huge dark spot, rather like Jupiter's Great Red Spot, that is larger than the earth.

These outer worlds of our solar system are obviously vastly different from earth. But there is an argument, albeit a slim one, for life. Scientists believe that water is present in the atmosphere of Jupiter, made up mainly of hydrogen and helium. There is also methane and ammonia —which, with water, could combine to form organic molecules associated with life. There could be some kind of creature swimming in the Jovian ocean or that of Uranus. But it could not be a civilized one in the way we understand it.

But our solar system is a grain of sand on the beach of the universe. Surely somewhere out there, in other solar systems around other stars, there are other worlds like earth where civilizations of some kind have developed?

According to Isaac Asimov, the reason why we may not have heard from such a civilization is basically one of distance. And inventing spaceships that simply go faster and faster is not the answer—the known laws of physics rule this out.

Above: Saturn and its rings, captured from a distance of 21 million miles by Voyager 1 in October 1980. The planet is visible through gaps in the rings. Note also the shadow of the planet on the rings, and of the rings on the planet.

Left: in close-up, the rings of Saturn, which appear continuous from afar, break up into a thousand or so individual ringlets. Particles in the rings are believed to consist of ice-covered rock, ranging in size from dust specks to boulders the size of office blocks.

Left: this montage of two Voyager 2 pictures shows in the foreground the distorted surface of the innermost large moon, Miranda. Beyond is the great blue-green ball of Uranus, the third largest planet, whose diameter is four times that of the earth.

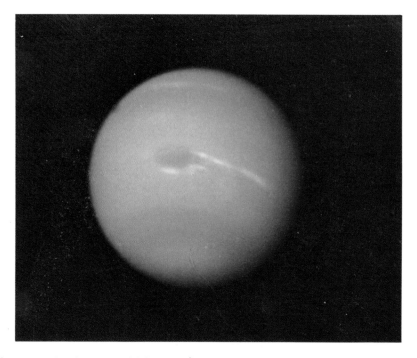

The planet Neptune, as seen by Voyager 2. In the middle of the disk is the Great Dark Spot, which is probably a huge storm center. The clouds are made up of crystals of methane ice.

Firstly, the acceleration needed to reach the very high speeds necessary would certainly kill the astronauts. A spaceship with an acceleration that could be tolerated would take at least four months to reach Venus; and a round trip to Mars would take a year. Once you think of leaving the solar system, even for the nearest star, Alpha Centauri (4.4 light years from earth), the time factor becomes intolerable. It is possible that astronauts could stand a slow acceleration, getting faster all the time, before reaching a maximum speed halfway between the planet of departure and arrival before decelerating. But again the laws of physics preclude very high speeds because the faster you go, the more energy needed to make you go faster is used to increase your mass. It was physicist Albert Einstein who first pointed out in his Special Theory of Relativity that it is impossible for any object with mass (and that obviously includes any spaceship) to exceed the speed of light.

Then why not travel at just below the speed of light? A nice idea—but really not possible, because, as a spaceship approaches the speed of light, so the energy needed to make it go faster would be used instead to increase its mass. When the speeds are high enough, so much energy goes into the mass and so little into additional speed that it really is not possible to go any faster. But if enough energy could be put aboard a spaceship to make it reach the speed of light—and allowing for acceleration and deceleration—it would take over 11 years for a return trip to Alpha Centauri.

"Physically" then, distance space travel must remain a dream. Unless, of course, we can find some way to work outside the known laws of physics. One idea is to convert the spaceship and all aboard into substances called photons—units of electromagnetic radiation which have "zero rest-mass." In other words, they do not have mass and are

Above: a space station of the future. An artist's impression of a ring-shaped space colony to house thousands of people. The ring would spin to provide artificial gravity on the inside of its outermost "wall."

not subject to the problem of increasing mass at increasing speed. Photons must, at all times, move through a vacuum at the speed of light.

When we speak of the speed of light, we actually mean that the photons are traveling at the speed of light, because light is made up of photons. So, if a way could be found to convert the spaceship and all aboard into photons, obviously the whole bundle would then shoot off immediately into space at the speed of light. Once the photons arrived at, say Alpha Centauri, they could be reconverted into the spaceship and crew. Even if this were possible—and scientists are nowhere near photon "conversion"—the space travelers would still be limited to the speed of light; and many of the stars in the Milky Way are thousands of light years from us.

Is there anything that goes faster than the speed of light? There might be. Some physicists believe that objects speculatively called tachyons might exist that cannot travel *below* the speed of light. Convert a spaceship into tachyons, and you could be at the other side of the galaxy in days. The trouble is that no one has so far detected a tachyon.

Above: inside the ring-shaped space colony shown above left. Conditions would be as earth-like as possible, with plants, lakes, normal air, houses and other buildings.

But in the absence of photon conversion and tachyon matter, is there not some other way of putting mankind across space? There seems to be only one—to load thousands of well-chosen volunteers into an enormous spaceship, which would have to be built in space because of its size, and wave goodbye to them forever.

Before that happens, man may have established whole colonies in space. Fortunately there is an ideal place for them to be: roughly the same orbit as our moon, but at equal distances from the moon and earth, forming an equilateral triangle. Thus the gravity of the moon and the earth would make sure a space colony would stay put in an orbit around the earth.

The American physicist Gerard O'Neill has suggested that settlements be built in these two "gravitational locks." The settlements could consist of cylinders, doughnut-shaped objects or spheres, big enough to hold 10,000 to 10 million people. Living inside their spinning artificial world, the inhabitants would have artificial gravity, controlled sunlight, enough air to produce sky, clouds, and rain. They could produce their own food from imported soil, their own industries, their own clothes. People would live out their whole lives in such space colonies.

Other such "libration" points would be discovered in the solar system until an extensive network of space colonies could be established. Eventually such a colony could leave the solar system altogether —and head out into space. Naturally, population growth would have to be controlled during such a voyage, which would take thousands of years to reach the nearest star. But the new astronauts would not be leaving home. They would be taking it with them, complete with food, air, and water supplies. Isaac Asimov describes such a space colony as a "free world" which, he postulates, would eventually, after many generations, approach a star—and if an earthlike planet could be found, either a new settlement could be founded, or contact made with the inhabitants of such a world.

If contact were made what would happen? Would there be a Star Wars battle in space? Or would the humans and the civilization they stumble upon combine to form a new understanding of the universe? Could it be that this will be mankind's ultimate voyage of discovery— the discovery that he is not alone, that he is part of a greater whole? The Russian founder of astronautics, K. E. Tsiolkovsky wrote in the opening years of this century, "Our planet is the cradle of reason, but one cannot live in a cradle forever."

Appendix

As space mission follows space mission, the names of successive astronauts and cosmonauts hold the headlines briefly—then become part of yesterday's news. In the years since Yuri Gagarin's historic flight in 1961, more than 100 human beings have already traveled in space. Some of them have gone up only once, some several times. Here, in the first pages of this appendix, is a record of some of these space pioneers, men and women, and their achievements.

This short biographical section is followed by a list of manned space flights. The Soviet Union achieved the first successful manned mission, when cosmonaut, Yuri Gagarin, orbited the earth in 1961, and it was a Russian who first walked in space—during the Voskhod 2 mission of 1965. An American astronaut, Neil Armstrong, was the first man to set foot on the moon—after Apollo 11 had landed on the lunar surface in 1969. The Soviet Union launched the world's first experimental space station in 1971. Two years later the American Skylab missions smashed all space duration records and proved that human beings can withstand long periods of weightlessness without suffering permanent harm.

July, 1975 saw a breakthrough in the spirit of international cooperation in space. After many months of preparation and practice missions, a successful joint Soviet-American venture culminated when Soyuz 19 docked with the final Apollo craft and their crews met in space.

Until 1978, only Russians and Americans took part in space flights. Then, in March that year, a Czech cosmonaut, Vladimir Remek, flew in Soyuz 28 and visited Salyut 6, and he has been followed by cosmonauts from Poland, East Germany, Bulgaria, Hungary, Vietnam, France and other countries.

Cosmonauts and astronauts are now surviving longer and longer periods in space—some cosmonauts have spent more than a year continuously in space in space station *Mir*. And the first reusable manned spacecraft—one capable of returning to earth again and again—the American Space Shuttle, was launched in April, 1981. It introduced an exciting new era in space transportation, although it has not proved as reliable or as cheap to operate as was hoped. The Soviet Union launched its first shuttle craft, *Buran*, in November, 1988. Shuttles will play a vital role in the construction of the international space station *Freedom* in the mid-1990's, which will provide the springboard for further exploration of the moon and beyond.

Left: this space photograph of earth shows Africa, the Mediterranean, the Red Sea (center), and southwestern Asia, and most strikingly, the swirling festoons of clouds in the earth's atmosphere. Already such pictures have proved to be of great scientific value, particularly in the study of world climates and weather, and more accurate, and timely weather forecasts are now possible. Future photographic studies may even help in the control of rainfall, and in the prediction of famine.

Astronauts and Cosmonauts

Some of the spacemen and women who made history

ARMSTRONG   ALDRIN   COLLINS

LOVELL   ANDERS   BORMAN

Aldrin, Edwin E., Jr. (1930—   ). United States astronaut, joined space program 1963. Flew Gemini 12 flight with James Lovell in 1966. Lunar module pilot on Apollo 11, the first moon-landing, July, 1969, and became second man to set foot on moon.

Allen, Joseph P. (1937—   ). United States astronaut, joined space program 1967. Mission specialist on Shuttle's first commercial flight, STS-5, during which two communications satellites were deployed. Spacewalked with Dale Gardner during the first satellite recovery mission 51-A.

Anders, William A. (1933—   ). United States astronaut, joined space program 1963. Flew Apollo 8 mission with Borman and Lovell, December, 1968, making 10 lunar orbits in course of 4-day flight.

Armstrong, Neil A. (1930—   ). United States astronaut, joined space program 1962. First space mission Gemini 8. Commander, Apollo 11. Became first man to walk on the moon, July 20, 1969, making "one small step for a man, one giant leap for mankind."

Bean, Alan L. (1932—   ). United States astronaut, joined space program 1963. Flew Apollo 12 mission in November, 1969, walking and working on lunar surface with Pete Conrad. Commanded second Skylab crew on 59-day flight in 1973.

Borman, Frank (1928—   ). United States astronaut, joined space program 1962. Copiloted Gemini 7, with James Lovell, circling earth 206 times, in two-week endurance-test mission. In December, 1968 he

POPOVICH   GAGARIN   TERESHKOVA   NIKOLAYEV   BYKOVSKY   G TITOV

commanded the Apollo 8 mission, which achieved the first manned circumnavigation of the moon in history.

Bykovsky, Valery F. (1934—   ). Soviet cosmonaut, began space training 1960 after training as test pilot. Piloted Vostok 5, launched June 14, 1963, for over 119 hours in orbit, landed by parachute June 19. Made 8-day flight in Soyuz 22, in September, 1966. Visited Salyut 6 space station for a week in August, 1978 on Soyuz 31 flight.

Carpenter, M. Scott (1925—   ). United States astronaut, joined space program in first group chosen, 1959. Became second American to orbit earth in May, 1962.

Cernan, Eugene A. (1934—   ). United States astronaut, joined space program 1963. Flew Gemini 9, June, 1966, with Tom Stafford, and moonshot "rehearsal," Apollo 10, May, 1969, with Stafford and John Young. Commanded the last lunar landing mission, Apollo 17, in December, 1972.

Chretien, Jean-Loup (1938—   ). French astronaut, began training in 1980 in France and Star City, Moscow. On Soyuz T-6 in June 1982, he became the first West European to go into space. On Soyuz TM-7, November 1988, he joined Musa Manarov and Vladimir Titov in *Mir*.

Collins, Michael (1930—   ). United States astronaut, joined space program 1963. Walked in space in course of first flight, Gemini 10, July, 1966, with John Young; piloted command module in Apollo 11 mission while Armstrong and Aldrin walked on the moon, July, 1969.

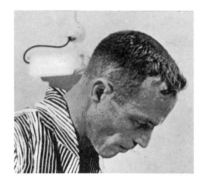

CARPENTER

CERNAN

CONRAD   GORDON   BEAN

COOPER

Conrad, Charles, Jr. (1930—   ). United States astronaut, joined space program 1962. Flew eight-day endurance test Gemini 5 flight, August, 1965. In November, 1969, commanded Apollo 12, second lunar landing mission. Commanded first Skylab crew in May, 1973.

Cooper, Leroy Gordon, Jr. (1927—   ). United States astronaut, joined space program in first group, 1959. First man to make two orbital flights: Mercury 9, alone, May 15, 1963; Gemini 5, with Conrad, August, 1965.

Crippen, Robert L. (1937—   ). United States astronaut, joined space program 1969. Pilot of *Columbia* on maiden flight of Space Shuttle, April 12, 1981. Commander of missions STS-7, 41-C, 41-G and 62-A. From 1988 Deputy Director Shuttle operations, Kennedy Space Center.

Fisher, Anna L. (1949—   ). One of the original six American woman astronauts, joined space program 1978. Flew as mission specialist on Shuttle mission 51-A. Married to fellow astronaut William F. Fisher (1946—   ), who first flew on 51-I.

Gagarin, Yuri A. (1934—1968). First human being to go into space. Cosmonaut, originally trained as test pilot. Made world's first space flight April 12, 1961 in Vostok 1. Circled earth once in 89 minutes. Died in airplane accident, 1968.

Gardner, Dale A. (1948—   ). United States astronaut, joined space program 1978. Flew on Shuttle missions STS-8 and 51-A, when spacewalking with Joseph Allen he took part in the daring mission to recover two communications satellites.

Garriott, Owen K. (1930—   ). United States astronaut, joined space program 1965. Took part in the second Skylab mission, 1973, remaining in space for 59 days. Mission specialist on maiden flight of Spacelab, November 1983.

Glenn, John H., Jr. (1921—   ). United States astronaut. Joined first space group in 1959. First American to enter earth orbit, piloting Mercury spacecraft Friendship 7 through three orbits in under five hours, after launch on February 20, 1962.

Grissom, Virgil I. (1926—1967). United States astronaut, joined space program 1959. First American to make more than one space flight. Piloted Mercury 4, July, 1961, copiloted two-man Gemini 3 flight, March 23, 1965, performing first orbital maneuvers by man in space. Died in Apollo fire, January 27, 1967.

Henize, Karl G. (1926—   ). United States astronaut, joined space program 1967. Mission specialist on Spacelab 2 flight, July 1985, when he became the oldest person (58) to go into space.

Jarvis, Gregory (1944—1986). United States astronaut, one of the crew of *Challenger* who perished when it exploded after liftoff on January 28, 1986.

Komarov, Vladimir M. (1927—1967). Soviet cosmonaut. First flight as part of three-man Voskhod 1 team, October 12, 1964. Died April 24, 1967, when Soyuz 1 crashed on re-entry.

Kubasov, Valeri N. (1935—   ). Soviet cosmonaut, first flew in Soyuz 6 in October, 1969. Flew with Leonov in Soyuz 19 for the Apollo-Soyuz link-up. In May, 1980, in Soyuz 36 visited the Salyut 6 space station with Bertalan Farkas, a Hungarian.

Leonov, Alexei A. (1934—   ). Soviet cosmonaut, became the first man to walk in space on March 18, 1965, spending 10 minutes outside Voskhod 2. Commanded Soyuz 19, the Soviet half of the Apollo-Soyuz joint mission in July, 1975.

GLENN

W FISHER   A FISHER

KOMAROV

LOVELL

Lovell, James A., Jr. (1928—   ). United States astronaut, joined space program in 1962. Flew Gemini 7, December, 1965, Gemini 12, November, 1966, and Apollo 8, December, 1968, then commanded Apollo 13 flight, April 11—17, 1970.

Lucid, Shannon W. (1943—   ). One of the original six American woman astronauts, joined space program in 1978. Mission specialist on Shuttle mission 51-G.

Manarov, Musakhi K. (1951—   ). Soviet cosmonaut, began training 1978. With Vladimir Titov became in December 1988 the first to spend more than a year in space (365 days 22 hr 39 min).

McAuliffe, S. Christa (1948—1986). Teacher who was scheduled on Shuttle mission 51-L to give the first lessons from space. Killed when *Challenger* exploded on January 28, 1986.

McCandless, Bruce (1937—   ). United States astronaut, joined space program 1966. As mission specialist on Shuttle mission 41-B made the first untethered spacewalk.

McNair, Ronald E. (1950—1986). United States astronaut, joined space program 1978. Mission specialist on Shuttle mission 41-B. Killed in the *Challenger* disaster, January 28, 1986.

Merbold, Ulf (1941—   ). West German astronaut. Payload specialist on Spacelab 1. First non-American to fly on an American spacecraft.

ONIZUKA   SMITH   MCAULIFFE   JARVIS   SCOBEE   RESNIK   MCNAIR

SHAW   MERBOLD   GARRIOTT   YOUNG

Onizuka, Ellison O. (1946—1986). United States astronaut, joined space program 1978. Mission specialist on Shuttle mission 51-C and 51-L, when he was killed in the *Challenger* tragedy, January 28, 1986.

Resnik, Judith A. (1949—1986). United States astronaut, joined space program 1978. Became the second American woman to enter space, on Shuttle mission 41-D, August 30, 1984. Killed on January 28, 1986, when *Challenger* exploded while taking off on 51-L.

Ride, Sally K. (1951—   ). Became the first American woman to go into space on STS-7, June 18, 1983. Joined space program 1978. Mission specialist on 41-G, the first space flight featuring two women (the other was Kathryn Sullivan). Married to astronaut Steven A. Hawley (1951—   ), who first went into space on 41-D.

Romanenko, Yuri V. (1944—   ). Soviet cosmonaut, began training 1970. First flew in space on Soyuz 26, December 1977. Missions also on Soyuz 38, September 1980, and Soyuz TM-2, February 1987. The latter flight ferried him to space station *Mir*, where he spent a record 326 days.

Ryumin, Valeri (1939—   ). Soviet cosmonaut, made two successive marathon flights aboard the Salyut 6 space station, spending 175 days aboard with Vladimir Lyakhov from February to August, 1979, and 185 days with Leonid Popov from April to October, 1980. This made him the world's most-traveled spaceman.

Savitskaya, Svetlana Y. (1948—   ). Soviet cosmonaut, began training 1980. On Soyuz T-7, August 1982, became the second woman to go into space. On Soyuz T-12, July 1984, became the first woman to make two space flights and the first to walk in space.

SCHIRRA

SHEPARD

Schirra, Walter Marty, Jr. (1923—   ). United States astronaut, joined space program in first group, 1959. Flew all three types of American spacecraft, starting with Mercury 8 mission, October, 1962. Copiloted Gemini 6 in first American rendezvous mission, with Gemini 7, December, 1965. Commander of Apollo 7 earth-orbital mission, October, 1968, with Eisele and Cunningham.

Scobee, F. Richard (1939—1986). United States astronaut, joined space program 1978. Pilot on Shuttle mission 41-C. Commander of *Challenger* on the ill-fated 51-L, when he perished in the explosion 73 seconds after liftoff.

Seddon, M. Rhea (1947—   ). One of the original six American woman astronauts, joined space program 1978. Mission specialist on Shuttle mission 51-D.

Shepard, Alan B., Jr. (1923—   ). United States astronaut, joined space program in first group, 1959. First American in space. Pilot of the first 15-minute suborbital Mercury flight, May 5, 1961. Commander of Apollo 14, February, 1971.

SULLIVAN   RIDE

STAFFORD

Smith, Michael J. (1945—1986). United States astronaut, joined space program 1980. Pilot of *Challenger* on Shuttle mission 51-L, and killed when the Orbiter exploded during launch.

Stafford, Thomas P. (1930—   ). United States astronaut, joined space program 1962. Four missions: Gemini 6, with Schirra, December, 1965; Gemini 9, with Cernan, June, 1966; Apollo 10, rehearsal for moonlanding, May, 1969; Apollo-Soyuz mission, July, 1975.

Sullivan, Kathryn D. (1951—   ). One of the original six American woman astronauts, joined space program 1978. As mission specialist on Shuttle mission 41-G, she made the first spacewalk by an American woman.

Tereshkova, Valentina Vladimirova (1937—   ). Soviet cosmonaut. First woman to travel in space. Piloted Vostok 6 in 48 orbits of earth, June 16 to June 19, 1963, coming within 3 miles of Vostok 5, launched June 14, 1963. Married cosmonaut Andrian Nikolayev in 1963.

Titov, Gherman, S. (1935—   ). Soviet cosmonaut. Began space training 1958, and became second Russian in space. Titov orbited earth 17 times in his 25 hours in space in August, 1961.

Titov, Vladimir G. (1947—   ). Soviet cosmonaut, began training 1976. Flew twice in space in 1983, in Soyuz T-8 and T-10; and with Musa Manarov in 1988 spent over 365 days in space in *Mir* to break the space duration record.

White, Edward H., II (1930—1967). United States astronaut, joined space program 1962. Flew Gemini 4 mission, 1965 with McDivitt, and became first American to walk in space. Died in Apollo fire, January 27, 1967.

Young, John W. (1930—   ). United States astronaut, joined space program 1962. Copiloted Gemini 3 with Grissom, 1965, piloted Gemini 10, July, 1966 while Collins walked in space. He was command module pilot of Apollo 10, May, 1969, the dress rehearsal for the first lunar landing mission. In April, 1972, flew as mission commander of Apollo 16. Commanded first orbital flight of Space Shuttle in 1981: in Orbiter *Columbia* with Robert Crippen. Commander of *Columbia* also on the first Spacelab flight, November 1988.

WHITE   McDIVITT

CRIPPEN   YOUNG

Chronology of
Manned Space Flights

MISSION	LAUNCH DATE	CREW
Vostok 1	April 12, 1961	Yuri Gagarin
Freedom 7	May 5, 1961	Alan Shepard (suborbital)
Liberty Bell 7	July 21, 1961	Virgil Grissom (suborbital)
Vostok 2	August 6, 1961	Gherman Titov
Friendship 7	February 20, 1962	John Glenn
Aurora 7	May 24, 1962	Scott Carpenter
Vostok 3	August 11, 1962	Andrian Nikolayev
Vostok 4	August 12, 1962	Pavel Popovich
Sigma 7	October 3, 1962	Walter Schirra
Faith 7	May 15, 1963	Gordon Cooper
Vostok 5	June 14, 1963	Valery Bykovsky
Vostok 6	June 16, 1963	Valentina Tereshkova
Voskhod 1	October 12, 1964	Vladimir Komarov, Konstantin Feoktistov, and Boris Egorov
Voskhod 2	March 18, 1965	Pavel Belyayev and Alexei Leonov
Gemini 3	March 23, 1965	Virgil Grissom and John Young
Gemini 4	June 3, 1965	James McDivitt and Edward White
Gemini 5	August 21, 1965	Gordon Cooper and Charles Conrad
Gemini 7	December 4, 1965	Frank Borman and James Lovell
Gemini 6	December 15, 1965	Walter Schirra and Thomas Stafford
Gemini 8	March 16, 1966	Neil Armstrong and David Scott
Gemini 9	June 3, 1966	Thomas Stafford and Eugene Cernan
Gemini 10	July 18, 1966	John Young and Michael Collins
Gemini 11	September 12, 1966	Charles Conrad and Richard Gordon
Gemini 12	November 11, 1966	James Lovell and Edwin Aldrin
Soyuz 1	April 23, 1967	Vladimir Komarov
Apollo 7	October 11, 1968	Walter Schirra, Donn Eisele, and Walter Cunningham
Soyuz 3	October 26, 1968	Georgi Beregovoi
Apollo 8	December 21, 1968	Frank Borman, James Lovell, and William Anders
Soyuz 4	January 14, 1969	Vladimir Shatalov
Soyuz 5	January 15, 1969	Evgeny Khrunov, Alexei Eliseyev, and Boris Volynov
Apollo 9	March 3, 1969	James McDivitt, David Scott, and Russell Schweickart
Apollo 10	May 18, 1969	Thomas Stafford, John Young, and Eugene Cernan
Apollo 11	July 16, 1969	Neil Armstrong, Michael Collins, and Edwin Aldrin

MISSION	LAUNCH DATE	CREW
Soyuz 6	October 11, 1969	Georgi Shonin and Valeri Kubasov
Soyuz 7	October 12, 1969	Anatoli Filipchenko, Vladislav Volkov, and Viktor Gorbatko
Soyuz 8	October 13, 1969	Vladimir Shatalov and Alexei Eliseyev
Apollo 12	November 14, 1969	Charles Conrad, Richard Gordon, and Alan Bean
Apollo 13	April 11, 1970	James Lovell, John Swigert, and Fred Haise
Soyuz 9	June 2, 1970	Andrian Nikolayev and Vitaly Sevastyanov
Apollo 14	January 31, 1971	Alan Shepard, Stuart Roosa, and Edgar Mitchell
Soyuz 10	April 23, 1971	Vladimir Shatalov, Alexei Eliseyev, and Nikolai Rukavishnikov
Soyuz 11	June 6, 1971	Georgi Dobrovolski, Viktor Patsayev, and Vladislav Volkov
Apollo 15	July 26, 1971	David Scott, Alfred Worden, and James Irwin
Apollo 16	April 16, 1972	John Young, Thomas Mattingly, and Charles Duke
Apollo 17	December 7, 1972	Eugene Cernan, Ronald Evans, and Harrison Schmitt
Skylab 2	May 25, 1973	Charles Conrad, Joseph Kerwin, and Paul Weitz
Skylab 3	July 28, 1973	Alan Bean, Owen Garriott, and Jack Lousma
Soyuz 12	September 27, 1973	Vasili Lazarev and Oleg Makarov
Skylab 4	November 16, 1973	Gerald Carr, Edward Gibson, and William Pogue
Soyuz 13	December 18, 1973	Pyotr Klimuk and Valentin Lebedev
Soyuz 14	July 3, 1974	Pavel Popovich and Yuri Artyukhin
Soyuz 15	August 26, 1974	Gennady Sarafanov and Lev Demin
Soyuz 16	December 2, 1974	Anatoli Filipchenko and Nikolai Rukavishnikov
Soyuz 17	January 11, 1975	Alexei Gubarev and Georgi Grechko
Soyuz 18	May 24, 1975	Pyotr Klimuk and Vitali Sevastyanov
Soyuz 19	July 15, 1975	Alexei Leonov and Valeri Kubasov
Apollo–Soyuz	July 15, 1975	Thomas Stafford, Vance Brand, and Donald Slayton
Soyuz 21	July 6, 1976	Boris Volynov and Vitaly Zholobov
Soyuz 22	September 15, 1976	Valery Bykovsky and Vladimir Aksenov
Soyuz 23	October 14, 1976	Vyacheslav Zudov and Valery Rozhdestvensky
Soyuz 24	February 7, 1977	Viktor Gorbatko and Yuri Glazkov
Soyuz 25	October 9, 1977	Vladimir Kovalyonok and Valeri Ryumin
Soyuz 26	December 10, 1977	Yuri Romanenko and Georgi Grechko
Soyuz 27	January 10, 1978	Vladimir Dzanibekov and Oleg Makarov
Soyuz 28	March 2, 1978	Alexei Gubarev and Vladimir Remek (Czech)

MISSION	LAUNCH DATE	CREW
Soyuz 29	June 15, 1978	Vladimir Kovalyonok and Alexander Ivanchenkov
Soyuz 30	June 27, 1978	Pyotr Klimuk and Miroslaw Hermaszewski (Polish)
Soyuz 31	August 26, 1978	Valery Bykovsky and Sigmund Jahn (East German)
Soyuz 32	February 25, 1979	Vladimir Lyakhov and Valeri Ryumin
Soyuz 33	April 10, 1979	Nikolai Rukavishnikov and Georgi Ivanov (Bulgarian)
Soyuz 35	April 9, 1980	Leonid Popov and Valeri Ryumin
Soyuz 36	May 26, 1980	Valeri Kubasov and Bertalan Farkas (Hungarian)
Soyuz T2	June 5, 1980	Yuri Malyshev and Vladimir Aksenov
Soyuz 37	July 23, 1980	Viktor Gorbatko and Pham Tuan (Vietnamese)
Soyuz 38	September 18, 1980	Yuri Romanenko and Arnaldo Mendez (Cuban)
STS-1, *Columbia*	April 12, 1981	John Young and Robert Crippen
Soyuz 40	May 15, 1981	Leonid I. Popov and Dumitru Prunariu
STS-2, *Columbia*	November 12, 1981	Joseph H. Engle and Richard H. Truly
STS-3, *Columbia*	March 22, 1982	Jack R. Lousma and Charles G. Fullerton
Soyuz T-5	May 13, 1982	Anatoli Berezovoi and Valentin V. Lebedev
Soyuz T-6	June 24, 1982	Vladimir A. Dzhanibekov, Alexander S. Ivanchenkov, and Jean-Loup Chretien
STS-4, *Columbia*	June 27, 1982	Thomas K. Mattingly and Henry W. Hartsfield
Soyuz T-7	August 19, 1982	Leonid I. Popov, Alexander A. Serebrov, and Svetlana Y. Savitskaya
STS-5, *Columbia*	November 11, 1982	Vance D. Brand, Robert F. Overmyer, William B. Lenoir, and Joseph P. Allen
STS-6, *Challenger*	April 4, 1983	Paul J. Weitz, Karol J. Bobko, F. Story Musgrave, and Donald H. Peterson
Soyuz T-8	April 20, 1983	Vladimir G. Titov, Gennadi M. Strekalov, and Alexander A. Serebrov
STS-7, *Challenger*	June 18, 1983	Robert L. Crippen, Frederick C. Hauck, John M. Fabian, Sally K. Ride, and Norman E. Thagard
Soyuz T-9	June 27, 1983	Vladimir A. Lyakhov and Alexander P. Alexandrov
STS-8, *Challenger*	August 30, 1983	Richard H. Truly, Daniel C. Brandenstein, Dale A. Gardner, Guion S. Bluford, and William E. Thornton
STS-9, *Columbia*	November 28, 1983	John W. Young, Brewster H. Shaw, Owen K. Garriott, Robert A. R. Parker, Ulf Merbold, and Byron K. Lichtenberg
STS 41-B, *Challenger*	February 3, 1984	Vance D. Brand, Robert L. Gibson, Bruce McCandless, Ronald E. McNair, and Robert L. Stewart
Soyuz T-10	February 8, 1984	Leonid D. Kizim, Vladimir A. Solovyov, Oleg Y. Atkov
Soyuz T-11	April 3, 1984	Yuri V. Malyshev, Gennadi M. Strekalov, Rakesh Sharma

MISSION	LAUNCH DATE	CREW
STS 41-C, *Challenger*	April 6, 1984	Robert L. Crippen, Francis R. Scobee, Terry J. Hart, George D. Nelson, and James D. A. van Hoften
Soyuz T-12	July 17, 1984	Vladimir A. Dzhanibekov, Svetlana Y. Savitskaya, and Igor P. Volk
STS 41-D, *Discovery*	August 30, 1984	Henry W. Hartsfield, Michael L. Coats, Steven A. Hawley, Judith A. Resnik, R. Michael Mullane, and Charles D. Walker
STS 41-G, *Challenger*	October 5, 1984	Robert L. Crippen, Jon A. McBride, Sally K. Ride, Kathryn D. Sullivan, David C. Leestma, Paul Scully-Power, and Marc Garneau
STS 51-A, *Discovery*	November 8, 1984	Frederick H. Hauck, David M. Walker, Dale A. Gardner, Joseph P. Allen, and Anna L. Fisher
STS 51-C, *Discovery*	January 24, 1985	Thomas K. Mattingly, Loren J. Shriver, Ellison S. Onizuka, James F. Buchli, and Gary Payton
STS 51-D, *Discovery*	April 12, 1985	Karol J. Bobko, Donald E. Williams, S. David Griggs, Jeffrey A. Hoffman, M. Rhea Seddon, Edwin Garn, and Charles D. Walker
STS 51-B, *Challenger*	April 29, 1985	Robert F. Overmyer, Frederick D. Gregory, Norman E. Thagard, William E. Thornton, Don L. Lind, Lodewijk van den Berg, and Taylor G. Wang
Soyuz T-13	June 6, 1985	Vladimir A. Dzhanibekov and Viktor P. Savinykh
STS 51-G, *Discovery*	June 17, 1985	John O. Creighton, John M. Fabian, Shannon W. Lucid, Steven R. Nagel, Patrick Baudry, and Prince Sultan A. A. Al-Saud
STS 51-F, *Challenger*	July 29, 1985	Charles G. Fullerton, Roy D. Bridges, Anthony W. England, Karl G. Henize, F. Story Musgrave, Loren W. Acton, and John-David Bartoe
STS 51-I, *Discovery*	August 27, 1985	Joseph H. Engle, Richard O. Covey, William F. Fisher, John M. Lounge, and James D. A. van Hoften
Soyuz T-14	September 17, 1985	Vladimir V. Vasyutin, Georgi M. Grechko, and Alexander A. Volkov
STS 51-J, *Atlantis*	October 3, 1985	Karol J. Bobko, Ronald J. Grabe, David C. Hilmers, Robert L. Stewart, and William Pailes
STS 61-A, *Challenger*	October 30, 1985	Henry W. Hartsfield, Steven R. Nagel, Guion S. Bluford, James F. Buchli, Bonnie J. Dunbar, Reinhard Furrer, Ernst W. Messerschmid, and Wubbo Ockels
STS 61-B, *Atlantis*	November 27, 1985	Brewster H. Shaw, Bryan D. O'Connor, Mary L. Cleave, Sherwood C. Spring, Jerry L. Ross, Rodolfo N. Vela, and Charles D. Walker

MISSION	LAUNCH DATE	CREW
STS 61-C, *Columbia*	January 12, 1986	Robert L. Gibson, Charles F. Bolden, Steven A. Hawley, George D. Nelson, Franklin R. Chang-Diaz, Robert J. Cenker, and C. William Nelson
STS 51-L, *Challenger*	January 28, 1986	Francis R. Scobee, Michael J. Smith, Judith A. Resnik, Ronald E. McNair, Ellison S. Onizuka, Gregory B. Jarvis, and S. Christa McAuliffe
Soyuz T-15	March 13, 1986	Leonid D. Kizim and Vladimir A. Solovyov
Soyuz TM-2	February 5, 1987	Yuri V. Romanenko and Alexander I. Leveikin
Soyuz TM-3	July 22, 1987	Alexander S. Viktorenko, Alexander P. Alexandrov, and Muhammad Faris
Soyuz TM-4	December 21, 1987	Vladimir G. Titov, Musakhi K. Manarov, and Anatoli S. Levchenko
Soyuz TM-5	June 7, 1988	Anatoli Y. Solovyov, Viktor P. Savinykh, and Alexander P. Alexandrov
Soyuz TM-6	August 29, 1988	Vladimir A. Lyakhov, Valeri Poliakov, and Abdul A. Mohmand
STS-26, *Discovery*	September 29, 1988	Frederick H. Hauck, Richard O. Covey, John M. Lounge, David C. Hilmers, and George D. Nelson
Soyuz TM-7	November 26, 1988	Alexander A. Volkov, Sergei Krikalev, and Jean-Loup Chretien
STS-27, *Atlantis*	December 2, 1988	Robert L. Gibson, Guy S. Gardner, Jerry L. Ross, R. Michael Mullane, and William M. Shepherd
STS-29, *Discovery*	March 13, 1989	Michael L. Coats, John E. Blaha, James P. Bagian, James F. Buchli, and Robert C. Springer
STS-30, *Atlantis*	May 4, 1989	David M. Walker, Ronald J. Grabe, Mary L. Cleave, Norman E. Thagard, and Mark C. Lee
STS-28, *Columbia*	August 8, 1989	Brewster H. Shaw, Richard N. Richards, Mark N. Brown, James C. Adamson, and David C. Leestma

Right: during Shuttle mission 51-A, on one of the most exciting spacewalks ever attempted, Dale Gardner fixes a "stinger" to the Westar communications satellite prior to jetting back with it to Orbiter *Discovery*. He is wearing and flying the MMU.

Index

food (diet) in space, 116–17, 123, 125, 133, 144–5
Fra Mauro, 116
Freedom 7 spacecraft, 53, 179
Freedom space station, 134, 135–7, 173
free-flying facility, 137
Friendship 7 spacecraft, 53, 179
fuel cells, 73, 76–7, 80, 113
fuel/propellant, specific impulse of, 41; liquid, 21, 24, 26, 29, 34, 36–7, 40, 41, 60, 141; solid, 21, 139, 141
Fullerton, Gordon, 144, 184, 185
Furrer, Reinhard, 185

G-force, 55, 56, 117, 146; *see also* gravity
Gagarin, Yuri, 48–9, 50–1, 55, 148, 173, 175, 176, 182
Galilei, Galileo, 14–15, 82, 83
Ganymede, 155, 163, 165
Gardner, Dale, 151–2, 176, 184, 185
Gardner, Guy, 186
Garn, Senator, 152, 185
Garneau, Marc, 185
Garriott, Owen, 126–8, 176, 179, 183, 184
Gemini spacecraft, 57, 73–9, 182; Gemini 3, 75, 76; Gemini 4, 75–6; Gemini 5, 76–7; Gemini 6, 77; Gemini 7, 75, 77; Gemini 8, 78; Gemini 9, 76, 78; Gemini 10, 78; Gemini 11, 78; Gemini 12, 78
Gemini-Titan spacecraft, 74
geophones, 116
geostationary orbits/satellites, 67
German Society for Space Travel, 31
Getaway Specials, 147
Gibson, Edward, 128, 183–4, 186
Gibson, Robert, 186
Glazkov, Yuri, 183
Glenn, John H. Jr, 53, 54–6, 176, 177, 182
Global Positioning System (GPS), 68; navigation satellite, 68
Goddard, Robert, 20, 26–9
Goddard Space Flight Center, USA, 26–7
Gorbatko, Viktor, 183, 184
Gordon, Richard, 78, 112, 176, 181, 182, 183
Grabe, Ronald, 185, 186
Gravitation, Newton's Law of Universal, 18, 40
gravity, discovery of, 18; magnification of, 56; of the moon, 82, 95; overcoming, 40–1, 126; *see also* G-force; weightlessness
Grechko, Georgi, 131–2, 183, 185
Gregory, Frederick, 185
Griggs, David, 185
Grissom, Virgil "Gus", 53, 55, 75–6, 91–100, 177, 182
Gubarev, Alexei, 132–3, 183, 184
Guggenheim, Daniel, 28
guided missiles, 34, 36–41
gyroscopes, 28, 34, 36, 40

habitation module, 137
Hadley Rille, 118
Haise, Fred, 112–13, 183
Halley, Edmund, 18
Ham, 48
Hart, Terry, 151, 185
Hartsfield, Henry, 184, 185
Hauck, Frederick, 184, 185, 186
Hawley, Steven, 185, 186

helium on Uranus, 166
Henize, Karl, 144, 177, 185
Hermaszewski, Miroslaw, 184
Hilmers, David, 185, 186
Hitler, Adolf, 33
Hoffman, Jeffrey, 152–3, 185
Hoften, James van, 151, 153, 185
Hornet, U.S.S., 110
Houston, Manned Spacecraft Center, 76, 95, 104, 113, 116; *see also* Mission Control
Hungarian cosmonauts, 133, 171
Hydar Ali, Prince, 22
hydrazine, as rocket fuel, 41
hydrogen, liquid, 41, 141; in Uranus' atmosphere, 166

infra-red photography, 67–8
instrument-carrying platform, 137
instrument module of Soyuz, 129
Intelsat, 64–5
intercontinental ballistic missile (ICBM), 58, 60
International Geophysical Year (IGY), 45, 46
International Telecommunication Satellite Corporation (Intelsat), 65
International Ultraviolet Explorer satellite, 71
interplanetary spacecraft, 137
Intrepid lunar module, 112
Io, 155, 163, 164, 165
iron, in moon soil, 94, 119; on Mars, 160, 161
Irwin, James, 103, 118, 183
Ivanchenkov, Alexander, 132, 184
Ivanov, Georgi, 132–3, 184

"J" missions, 116–18
Jahn, Sigmund, 184
Jarvis, Gregory, 177, 178, 186
Juno 1 rocket, 46
Jupiter, 15, 155, 162–5
Jupiter missile, 45

Kennedy, John F., 73
Kennedy Space Center, Florida, 103, 110, 146, 147, 148
Kepler, Johannes, 16–17
Kerwin, Joseph, 123–6, 183
Khrunov, Evgeny, 182
Kitty Hawke command module, 116
Kizim, Leonid, 135, 184, 186
Klimuk, Pyotr, 131, 183, 184
Kohoutek comet, 128
Komarov, Vladimir M., 58, 92–3, 128, 177, 182
Kovalyonok, Vladimir, 132, 183, 184
Krakow, 12–14
Krikalev, Sergei, 186
Kubasov, Valeri N., 131, 177, 183, 184

laboratory module, 137; *see also* Spacelab
Laika, 46
Landsats, 67–8, 71
laser, 107
launch escape system, 135
lava flows, lunar, 83–4; *see also* volcanoes
Lazarev, Vasili, 183
Leasat satellite, 152–3
Lebedev, Valentin, 134, 183, 184
Lee, Mark, 186
Leestma, David, 185, 186
Lenoir, William, 184

Leonov, Alexei, 60, 61, 75, 130–1, 177, 182, 183
Levchenko, Anatoli, 186
Leveikin, Alexander, 186
Liberty Bell 7 spacecraft, 53, 182
Lichtenberg, Byron, 142, 184
light, speed of, 8, 166, 168
Lind, Don, 185
Lounge, John, 185, 186
Lousma, Jack, 126–8, 183, 184
Lovell, James A. Jr, 77, 78, 93, 95, 112–13, 178, 182, 183
Lucid, Shannon, 178, 185
Luna (Lunik) spacecraft, Luna I, 47, 84–5; Luna 2, 85; Luna 3, 47, 85; Luna 9, 87; Luna 10, 87; Luna 15, 103; Luna 16, 89; Luna 20, 89; Luna 24, 89
lunar modules (LM), 74, 79, 80–2, 93, 97, 98–101, 103–9, 112
Lunar Orbiters *see* Orbiter spacecraft; Surveyor spacecraft
lunar rover, 116–17
lunar roving vehicle (lunar rover), 117–18, 119–21
lunar spacecraft, 137
Lunokhod lunar rover, 89
Lyakhov, Vladimir, 132–3, 184, 186

McAuliffe, Christa, 178, 186
McBride, Jon, 185
McCandless, Bruce, 150–1, 178, 184
McDivitt, James A., 75, 91, 97, 98–9, 181, 182
McNair, Robert, 178, 184, 186
Makarov, Oleg, 183
Malyshev, Yuri, 184
Manarov, Musa, 135, 178, 186
manned maneuvering unit, 150–1
Manned Spacecraft Center, 76; *see also* Houston; Mission Control
manned space flight, American, 53–8, 73–84, 92–101, 103–31, 182–6; Russian, 48–9, 56–61, 92–3, 128–33, 182–6
maria (lunar seas), 82, 83–4, 85, 87, 89
Mariner space probes, Mariner 4, 158–60; Mariner 6, 158; Mariner 7, 158; Mariner 9, 158–61; Mariner 10, 157
Mars, 15–16, 17, 133, 158–61, 169; manned bases on, 137
mascons, 89
mass ratio of rocket, 41–2
materials research in space, 126, 131, 143
Mattingly, Thomas, 118, 119, 183, 184, 185
medical problems of space flights, 74, 76, 77, 116–17, 128, 133
Mendez, A. T., 133, 184
Merbold, Ulf, 142, 143, 178, 179, 184
Mercury, 157–8
Mercury-Atlas rocket, 48, 53, 58, 60
Mercury-Redstone rocket, 48
Mercury spacecraft, 44, 45, 53, 58–60, 73, 147, 182; Mercury 3, 55, 75; Mercury 6, 55; Mercury 9, 74
Messerschmid, Ernst, 185
meteorites, 88
meteoroid/sun shield, for Skylab, 123, 125
meteoroids, 116, 123, 125; on Martian surface, 158; on moon surface, 82–3, 84, 119, 120
Meteosat, 66
methane, in Uranus' atmosphere, 166

Picture Credits

Listed below are the sources of all the illustrations in this book.

Aldus Archives, 25(t); Rudolph Britto © Aldus Books, 112; Peter Cook © Aldus Books, 21, 40, 58, 75(b), 78, 85, 96(t), 109; Geoffrey Drury © Aldus Books, 9; John Freeman © Aldus Books, 11; M. Jaanus © Aldus Books, 24(b), 36; John Messenger © Aldus Books, 18(b), 19(b); Archivio di Stato, Moderna, 14; Office of the Assistant Secretary of Defense, Washington D.C., 41; Associated Press Ltd, 20, 88(r); The Astronomer Royal for Scotland/Photo J. B. Watson Ltd, Edinburgh, 16(t); Johannes Kepler, Astronomia Nova 1609, 17(br); Tycho Brahe, Astronomiae Instauratae 1648, 16(b); Barnaby's Picture Library, 44, 94, 100, 107; Biblioteca Nazionale Centrale, Florence, 82(b); P. Bono and K. Gatland, Frontiers of Space, Blandford Press Ltd, London 1969, 59; the Trustees of the British Museum, 8(b), 10, 17(tr); British Museum/Photo John Freeman © Aldus Books, 8(t); Camera Press, 132(l,r), 133; Gerald Davis © 1981 Contact Press Images/Colorific, 138; Fondation Saint-Thomas, Strasbourg, 17(l); Mrs. Robert H. Goddard, 27; Mrs. Robert H. Goddard/ Photo by B. Anthony Stewart © National Geographic Society, 28; Holiday Film Corporation/Space Frontiers, 135, 141, 142(t), 146; Hughes Aircraft Corporation, 88(l); the Jet Propulsion Laboratory, California Institute of Technology, sponsored by NASA, 87(l,r); Keystone, 32; Erich Lessing— Magnum Photos, 12, 13; Meteosat Data Service/Science Photo Library, 66; Director General, Monumenti, Musei e Gallerie Pontificie, Photographic Archives of the Vatican Museums and Galleries, 83(t); National Aeronautics & Space Administration, Washington D.C., 6, 7, 30, 52, 64(r), 70(r), 72, 74, 75(t), 76(l,r), 79, 80, 86, 90, 93(l), 95, 98, 102, 104, 105(t), 106, 108, 110, 111, 113(l,r), 118, 120, 124, 125, 127(b), 129, 157, 160(t), 161, 162, 165(b), 167(t,b), 170(l,r), 172, 174(t,b), 176(t,b), 178(t), 180(t); NASA/Colorific, 62, 156(t), 164; NASA/Science Photo Library, 69(t), 70(l), 119, 121(t,b), 122, 126, 130, 154, 156(b), 159, 163, 165(t); NASA/Spacecharts, 134, 136, 137, 140, 142(b), 144, 145, 147, 149, 150, 152, 168, 177(bl), 178(b), 179(t), 180(c), 181(b); National Air and Space Museum, Smithsonian Institution, Washington D.C., 26; National Portrait Gallery, London, 18(t); Woolsthorpe Manor, a property of the National Trust/Photo David Swann © Aldus Books, 19(t); © New York Herald Tribune, 48(br); Novosti, 48(tl), 56(tr), 57, 60, 84, 89, 93(r), 175(t), 177(br); Novosti and Opera Mundi, 77; Novosti/Spacecharts, 153; Picturepoint, London, 23, 99, 114(all), 117; Photri, 127(t), 158; Popperfoto, 39(b), 50, 54; Rockwell International (Space Division)/Science Photo Library, 68; the Royal Asiatic Society, 22; Science (The Macdonald Illustrated Library) Macdonald & Co. (Publishers) Ltd, © Rathbone Books Limited, London 1960, 82(t); Science Photo Library, 64(l); Spacecharts, 63, 67, 69(b), 151, 169, 187; Space Frontiers, 128(t,b), 160(b); Photo David Swann © Aldus Books by courtesy Science Museum, London, 83(b); Society for the Cultural Relations with the USSR, 56(tl), 85; Stern Archiv, Hamburg, 25(b), 31(c,b), 34, 35(t,b), 37; Stern-Seeliger, 53; Fotohronika Tass, 24(t), 46, 49, 61; Uffize, Florence/ Photo Scala, 15; U.P.I., 33; Ullstein Bilderdienst, 39(t); United States Information Service, London, 43, 47, 92(l), 97(b), 107(b), 175(c,b), 177(t), 179(b), 180(b), 181(t)